52-WEEK

NEWLYWED
COUPLE'S
DEVOTIONAL

52-WEEK
NEWLYWED
COUPLE'S
DEVOTIONAL

PRAYERS TO GROW
YOUR FAITH AND LOVE

Dr. Chavonne Perotte

ROCKRIDGE
PRESS

Copyright © 2022 by Rockridge Press, Oakland, California

THE HOLY BIBLE, NEW INTERNATIONAL VERSION®, NIV® Copyright © 1973, 1978, 1984, 2011 by Biblica, Inc.® Used by permission. All rights reserved worldwide.

No part of this publication may be reproduced, stored in a retrieval system, or transmitted in any form or by any means, electronic, mechanical, photocopying, recording, scanning, or otherwise, except as permitted under Sections 107 or 108 of the 1976 United States Copyright Act, without the prior written permission of the Publisher. Requests to the Publisher for permission should be addressed to the Permissions Department, Rockridge Press, 1955 Broadway, Suite 400, Oakland, CA 94612.

Limit of Liability/Disclaimer of Warranty: The Publisher and the author make no representations or warranties with respect to the accuracy or completeness of the contents of this work and specifically disclaim all warranties, including without limitation warranties of fitness for a particular purpose. No warranty may be created or extended by sales or promotional materials. The advice and strategies contained herein may not be suitable for every situation. This work is sold with the understanding that the Publisher is not engaged in rendering medical, legal, or other professional advice or services. If professional assistance is required, the services of a competent professional person should be sought. Neither the Publisher nor the author shall be liable for damages arising herefrom. The fact that an individual, organization, or website is referred to in this work as a citation and/or potential source of further information does not mean that the author or the Publisher endorses the information the individual, organization, or website may provide or recommendations they/it may make. Further, readers should be aware that websites listed in this work may have changed or disappeared between when this work was written and when it is read.

For general information on our other products and services or to obtain technical support, please contact our Customer Care Department within the United States at (866) 744-2665, or outside the United States at (510) 253-0500.

Rockridge Press publishes its books in a variety of electronic and print formats. Some content that appears in print may not be available in electronic books, and vice versa.

TRADEMARKS: Rockridge Press and the Rockridge Press logo are trademarks or registered trademarks of Callisto Media Inc. and/or its affiliates, in the United States and other countries, and may not be used without written permission. All other trademarks are the property of their respective owners. Rockridge Press is not associated with any product or vendor mentioned in this book.

Interior and Cover Designer: Tricia Jang
Art Producer: Sara Feinstein
Editor: Adrian Potts
Production Editor: Jenna Dutton
Production Manager: Martin Worthington

Illustration used under license from Shutterstock. Author photo courtesy of Jasmine Alston Photography.

Paperback ISBN: 978-1-68539-148-5
eBook ISBN: 978-1-68539-222-2
R0

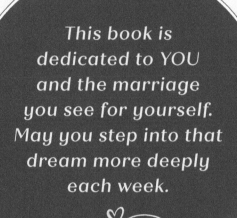

This book is
dedicated to YOU
and the marriage
you see for yourself.
May you step into that
dream more deeply
each week.

CONTENTS

INTRODUCTION

Congratulations! On your marriage, on the life you envision together, and on the wisdom to invest your precious time into nurturing your bond. You are already setting yourself up for massive success. When you think about the day you married, the marriage vows and celebration, it's probably pretty evident that you entered a sacred covenant with God and each other. But that sacredness is also something that many couples lose sight of as their day-to-day lives take over, when unmet expectations surface and unexpected new challenges land in their laps.

In the pages of this devotional, you will find the perspective, wisdom, insight, and tools you need to navigate many of the things you will encounter as a new couple. Each week, you will grow stronger and deeper in your relationship with God, in your connection to His work, and in your understanding of and love for each other. You will also be presented with ideas to think about and apply in your regular interactions. It's important to remember that the tiny, daily decisions are what build the marriage of your dreams. And you are already on your way.

As a marriage and life coach for couples, I see daily the struggles common to many marriages. It's not until things are too frustrating or disappointing that many seek my help. I help them untangle wrong thinking, heal hurt feelings, and establish productive new habits of interacting with each other. And over the course of several months, they find themselves in a much better place, enjoying their marriage and full of confidence that they are back on the right track. I'm honored to spend this time with you, showing you what to focus on now so that your marriage doesn't encounter the hardships that can be avoided by having the right perspective and information. It is my hope that you start your marriage being equipped with a healthy dose of reality, tools to help you express your ideas in healthy ways, and a firm footing in God's Word as a guide.

I often look at a photo of my husband and me on our wedding day. We had an ideal courtship and never doubted our relationship with each other. But over time, as challenges presented themselves and when we didn't have the tools we do now, we really struggled to connect, communicate, and operate well as a team. Even as we attend weddings now, we both knowingly look at each other, praying for the best while also knowing that most couples don't understand what really lies ahead for them.

By reading this devotional and applying its wisdom, you will know, and you will have the support and spiritual insight to overcome anything life or marriage may throw your way. This book is a divine appointment. Approach each devotion with an open mind, heart, and eyes, ready to experience what it is God wants you to know, feel, see, and do. Your marriage will benefit greatly.

BLESSINGS TO YOU AND A LIFETIME OF FULFILLING LOVE!

HOW TO USE THIS DEVOTIONAL

This devotional is organized into 52 weeks with four core themes—cooperation, communication, conflict, and love. Each week's devotion includes relevant scripture, reflections, discussion questions, and practical action items. Remember: There is no right or wrong way to use this book. Work from start to finish, or move around each week as you are drawn to particular topics. Be led by whatever you need most at the time.

I recommend you work through this devotional together, whether you read it at the same time or share turns and then come together to discuss. Knowing that your partner is reading and digesting the information alongside you will strengthen your connection and your closeness.

The time needed to study and discuss each week's devotion ranges from 10 to 20 minutes, depending on the depth of conversation you have. The action items can be easily integrated into your daily life and provide an added boost to your relationship. You can dedicate a specific day each week to this devotional or approach the schedule in a more flexible way. The experience you have should be led by a desire to grow closer together and to God and not by an obligation to finish as quickly as possible. Get all that you need out of it.

Your investment of time will reap huge rewards in your faith, love, and understanding of each other. God is already pleased and is smiling down as He sees your heart and desire to make your marriage successful. And if God is for you, who can be against you? (Romans 8:31)

COOPERATING AS A COUPLE

Cooperating as a couple is something you're already equipped to do, but being intentional about cooperation together will build your skills. Great marriages don't just happen— they are created. In part 1, you will explore several topics necessary for you to function well as a couple for a lifetime.

WHY BE YOUR BEST?

To do what is right and just is more acceptable
to the Lord than sacrifice.

PROVERBS 21:3

What motivates you to show up the way you do in your marriage?
Is it because it is expected of you? Because it makes your partner
happy? Or is it out of habit and what feels familiar?

One of the most valuable things you can do as you start your
marriage is deeply question *why* you do what you do. Functioning as
a couple requires that you understand your intentions and motiva-
tions. When you are doing things just because it's what your partner
wants, you lose your internal motivation. This can lead to resentment, as you deny what is right for you. Alternatively, when you do
things out of habit, you don't ever uncover if it represents the standard God has set for you. You miss out on the opportunity to stretch
and grow into all that He created you to be.

Why you want to be a good partner and function well as a couple
may seem like an insignificant question to ask. Most people respond
with "Because I love my partner" or "It's just what a person should
do." Go deeper and think about how you show up as an offering to
God. Doing what is right comes from a place of personal integrity
and glorifies the Lord. There will be times in your marriage when
you don't want to do things because you don't feel a compelling love
for your partner or you don't agree it's something you should do.
God's Word should be a compass in these moments.

REFLECTIONS

- What is the reason you want to be a great partner in this marriage, and how can you keep that in the forefront of your mind during challenging times? Where does God fit into that reason? How can you rely on His help, wisdom, and insight when you struggle to show up as your best?

- Reflect on a time when you fell short of being your best as a partner and what happened in that situation. How would being clear about *why* you wanted to do better have helped you in that moment?

WORKING TOGETHER THIS WEEK

☐ List seven qualities you want to embody as a couple. Write down the reasons the qualities are important and how they honor God's design for your union. From the list, identify the one area in which each of you struggles the most. Discuss ways you can support each other as you grow in these areas.

☐ There will be days in your marriage when you're angry and frustrated with each other, yet you can commit now to showing up as your best. Take turns completing this sentence as a statement of your commitment: "Even when I'm very upset with you, I am committed to being a good partner because _____."

☐ When God looks down and sees how you're showing up as a partner to each other, what do you want Him to be able to say? In what ways do you want to make God proud? Take a moment now to affirm each other in those statements. For example, Partner A should say aloud the things Partner B would like God to see in them, and vice versa.

REAL COMMITMENT

Commit to the Lord whatever you do, and he
will establish your plans.

PROVERBS 16:3

Marriage is a commitment, a covenant, a promise to stay together
and to keep trying. Yet we have no idea what we are *really* committing to. There will always be circumstances in life that take us off
guard, things we will come to know about our partner that are disappointing, and issues within ourselves that bring a lot of things into
question. This is why our commitment should first be to the Lord.

God is unchanging and all-knowing. No matter what may take us
by surprise, it is already known by God, and He has a plan for getting
through. In marriage, a commitment to God means you look to Him
for the reason to keep going when your own motivation wanes. And
it *will* wane. We are all human beings living in response to our reality.
Yet when we can take our eyes and minds to a higher place in God,
we can trust and rely on Him to carry us over the momentary hurdles into the ultimate vision for our union.

As a newly married couple, there are many things you are adjusting to right now. As you discover yourself, you discover your partner.
You are also discovering more and more about God. His commitment
to you makes it easier for you to be committed to Him. The same
principle operates in your marriage. For your marriage to thrive, you
should constantly commit to be committed. To the process. To the
learning. To the growth. And, yes, even to the challenges.

REFLECTIONS

- How are we committing our marriage to the Lord right now, and what are some areas where we can show even greater commitment? What would be different if we were operating at the highest level of commitment?

- What are the things we want God to establish in our marriage, and what internal and external goals do we want to achieve? What will commitment look like when we struggle in those goals? Why will we want to remain committed, and how can God help?

WORKING TOGETHER THIS WEEK

☐ Together, create your own commitment statement by completing the following prompts:

To you, Lord, I commit _____.

To my partner, I commit _____.

To myself, I commit _____.

☐ Write a list of three things you want God to do in your marriage right now. Decide now to offer your thoughts, feelings, and actions to God as your commitment to achieving those things. What specific shifts do you know you need to make in order for those desires to manifest? What will you need to start doing differently? What will you need to stop doing?

☐ Share with each other one thing you have personally done a good job of committing to. What made you successful? What things did you tell yourself? What actions did you take, and how did they evolve over time? What similarities do you notice in your approaches? What lessons learned in that experience can be applied here to your marriage?

BUILDING A VISION

For the revelation awaits an appointed time;
it speaks of the end and will not prove false.
Though it linger, wait for it; it will certainly
come and will not delay.

HABAKKUK 2:3

As you united as a couple, each of you had a vision for how your marriage would unfold. There are experiences you want to have together, a certain life you want to build. Whatever you have in mind requires your teamwork, perseverance, and patience to see it through. There is your timeline, and there is God's. Often, in the building of a vision together, you are unaware of all that will be required and all that will hold up your progress along the way. This verse is a helpful anchor in keeping your faith.

I think about my own first anniversary trip, during which my husband and I mapped out our plans to buy a house and have a child. Buying the house was easy, and we stayed right on track. But having a child took a bit longer and was much more complicated than either of us anticipated. Yet, in God's wisdom, everything was right on time.

You will have your own delays as you walk out your marriage vision. You should remind yourself of what you are working toward together and understand the role each of you can play. You should also be open to certain aspects of your vision coming to pass in unexpected ways. It's always exciting to talk about your goals and dreams. Be sure to find that same enthusiasm as you are taking the daily actions and steps to realize that goal. Be conscious of how you want to treat and be there for each other when things don't go according to plan.

REFLECTIONS

- Reflect on the goals you have for your marriage and how informed they are by the Word of God. What would God say about your vision? How might it glorify Him and His purposes here on earth? If you have left God out of the picture, how can you include Him more?

- What stands out to you most from this week's scripture, and where has it already proven itself true in your life? How did you manage any waiting period you experienced, and what lessons did you learn that will help you as a couple now? How can you both support each other as you walk and wait for aspects of your marriage vision to take place?

WORKING TOGETHER THIS WEEK

☐ What are three things you'd like to accomplish as a couple? Discuss why those things are important to you and establish a timeline for when you'd like to accomplish the goals. What are some obstacles that might get in the way? What will you do if it takes longer? Write out a Plan B and include specific ways in which you will trust God in His timing.

☐ Identify something that has already taken longer to happen for you as a couple and how you feel about the situation. How have you supported each other? Is there anything you could be doing differently or better right now?

☐ Carve out some time to pray together and offer your vision to God. Ask that He show you what He wants for you and that He give you the desires of His heart. Open your mind to see things on a higher level, and seek His wisdom and guidance.

KNOWING YOUR VALUES

Let us examine our ways and test them, and let us return to the Lord.

LAMENTATIONS 3:40

How well do you know yourself? Self-awareness is an essential skill when it comes to creating and sustaining a healthy marriage. You and your partner are always doing a dance with each other that is based on your own thoughts, ideas, opinions, preferences, and values. Knowing what is important to both of you and why will help you both understand the choices you make and how you react to each other.

In a marriage, you will each naturally value different things. This is partly due to your upbringing and how you were socialized. For example, one of you may value discipline and the other may value fun. Neither is right or wrong. The only way you can come to that understanding is by first knowing yourself. What are the things you value? How does the way you spend your time, energy, and resources reflect your values? Are you consciously choosing the things you value, or do they feel like things that are imposed upon you?

God has designed your brain to be able to think deeply about what is happening and to allow you to watch your own thoughts *while* it is happening. This is the way you examine yourself. The Holy Spirit is within you, also directing and pointing you to what is right thinking. This is the way you test what you are thinking and feeling against the will and word of God. When you notice a gap in these things, you have the opportunity to anchor yourself and return to God.

REFLECTIONS

- Have you ever spent time thinking about the things you value? What was it like to consider your values and how they show up in your marriage? How will considering what you value help you operate better as a couple? How might knowing your values make it challenging for you as a couple?

- What do you think God values? What are the things He might value most about marriage and want you to experience? What is one value you believe you and your partner are already living out well?

WORKING TOGETHER THIS WEEK

☐ Create a values map. Each person makes a chart that includes three columns. For the first column, write out a list of your top five values. These can be anything from tangible items like people and things to intangible qualities and internal traits.

☐ In the second column, link the things you value to specific situations and circumstances where your values are evident. For example, if you value fun, how do you live that out? What do you do to express your value of fun? How do you feel and react when you are not able to operate from your values?

☐ In the third column, ask God to show you where your values align with His. Seek His wisdom in how you prioritize the things you value and in identifying ways to make sure they are balanced. Spend time thinking about if any of your values are in conflict with each other.

Note: The information you uncover here will be used next week as you work together with your partner. For now, these are individual exercises to work through on your own.

YOUR PARTNER'S VALUES

And let us consider how we may spur one
another on toward love and good deeds, not
giving up meeting together, as some are in the
habit of doing, but encouraging one another . . .

HEBREWS 10:24–25

There may be many things you know about your partner, but many
more things are still to be learned. In marriage, you want to exist in a
state of wonder and curiosity about each other. It's what fueled your
getting to know each other in the beginning. Part of what will make
your marriage successful is to be intentional about studying each
other. To love your partner well, you want to understand what they
value and find important in life.

When you are aware of what moves and inspires your partner,
you can be the proper support in encouraging them. Your efforts will
be more effective and well received. You were brought together to
create an experience that's better together than apart. This verse is
a wonderful reminder of how the point of being a couple is to help
each other love more and do more good, both in your own home and
in the world.

Knowing what your partner values also enables you to better
understand your differences and find more productive ways to
resolve issues. You uncover that their actions are more about them
and their priorities and less about intentionally dismissing what's
important to you. When you take the time to learn more about each
other, you'll make fewer assumptions and judge each other less.
Now is a great time to dive deeper into understanding the desires
and values God put into your partner and how they can help your
marriage grow.

REFLECTIONS

- Do you value knowing your partner better? What are some areas you'd like to learn more about? What gets in the way of you having deeper and more intimate conversations with each other, and what would make it easier to share more of your authentic selves?

- How do you see each other's values already working together to make your marriage better? How might some of your values and priorities be in conflict with each other? What needs to happen so you can be more on the same page? What would God advise you to do?

WORKING TOGETHER THIS WEEK

☐ Taking what we uncovered about your own values last week, share your insights with your partner. Give them one or two specific examples of how you've seen your own values show up in your relationship together. Then listen as they share theirs. What common themes do you notice? Anything that surprises either of you? Anything you can learn from each other?

☐ Express an appreciation for each other by sharing with your partner one way you see God using them in your family or in the world right now. Highlight one of their values that you really admire and why you are grateful God designed them that way.

☐ Decide on three specific values that you want for yourselves as a couple. This may be a combination of your individual values, or you may decide on new ones altogether. Search through scripture and find a verse that represents how you want to operate as a couple, keeping in mind the values you've selected.

BEING TEAMMATES

From him the whole body, joined and held
together by every supporting ligament, grows
and builds itself up in love, as each part does
its work.

EPHESIANS 4:16

In your marriage, each of you has an important role to play. It's the bringing together of your unique talents and roles that will help you function best as a couple. You are a cohesive team interdependent on each other. As this scripture reveals, God has created all of us to work together, supporting each other, growing, and increasing in love as we go about our purposes. The marriage union can be a phenomenal example of this at work.

One key to you both being able to operate at a high level as a team is to be conscious to grow and build yourselves up in love. When you first get together, the falling-in-love part is easy. It may feel like it just happened to you. But when you're married, over time, being in love, growing in love, and supporting each other in love will be much more intentional and conscious. There will be times when you let each other down, and the appropriate response will be to lean into love rather than criticism. When your focus is on supporting each other and you see yourselves as extensions of each other, you will abound in grace.

When you focus on truly supporting each other, working together well is an automatic by-product. You rely on each other's strengths and fill in the gaps to each other's weaknesses. You don't judge each other for any gaps in skills but instead think creatively about how to make sure you are working and loving each other well.

REFLECTIONS

- What stands out to you most about this week's verse? What's the message in it for you? In what ways are you an example of this idea in your marriage right now? In what ways is your partner an example of this idea?

- What are your current strengths as a couple? What mindset and skills have helped you work well as a team so far? Where are your areas for continued growth? Where can God support you both more? If you saw yourself as a three-person team becoming extraordinary together, what would each of you be working on right now?

WORKING TOGETHER THIS WEEK

☐ Using this scripture as a reference, come up with your own definition of what it means to be a team in your marriage. What would it look like on the outside, and how would you be thinking and feeling on the inside?

☐ Identify one way you can be a better team member to your partner in the coming week. Find one thing you will start doing or stop doing so you work well together. For example, you might be more intentional about having a daily check-in to discuss your plans or needs for the day and how you both can accommodate each other's schedules. Think about what would motivate you to carry this out and how it aligns with your value and the person you know God wants you to be.

☐ Come up with one personal weakness you could use some help with. Offer that weakness to God in a prayer. Ask Him to use your partner as a support system as you grow and become better in that area. Let your partner know of one specific way they can help you.

THE COMMON GOAL

> Therefore if you have any encouragement from
> being united with Christ, if any comfort from his
> love, if any common sharing in the Spirit, if any
> tenderness and compassion, then make my joy
> complete by being like-minded, having the same
> love, being one in spirit and of one mind.

PHILIPPIANS 2:1–2

What's the point of your marriage? Have you ever asked yourself this question? There are your answers, your partner's answers, and, of course, God's answers. In all likelihood, you will approach things in very different ways. That's okay. In marriage, you do not need to be carbon copies of each other thinking the same thoughts all the time. Instead, you want to focus always on your common goal.

A mentor of mine once made the statement that the point of marriage is to love. I think God has been showing us this truth in His word since the very beginning. What if you lived your life together as if the only point was to love each other deeply? When you keep the common goal of love in mind, you more easily accept each other and offer a gracious, consistent love. If both of you are doing this to your highest capacity, there will be no lack in your marriage.

Many couples face challenges when they forget love, focus on their individual agendas, and become too preoccupied with themselves. Many people spend time making marriage something that it's not. They work to get their partner to do the things they want, say the things they want, become the things they want. But in the process, they don't see how they are not loving their partners fully and unconditionally. Love is the greatest unifier in the world. It is a powerful force that makes you unstoppable as a couple.

REFLECTIONS

- What is your personal definition of love? How does this compare to God's definition of love as patient, kind, and so on (1 Corinthians 13: 4–7)? How often do you find love being the center of your thoughts and actions in your marriage? What would help you keep this as the common goal more often? What would it look like if you did?

- How has God been the perfect example of the common goal of love? Exchange your own specific examples of how God is love-track minded—meaning, how He only focuses on love. What can He teach you in this area? What's a moment in time in your relationship when you could have really used this lesson and done things differently?

WORKING TOGETHER THIS WEEK

☐ Come up with a statement together that helps remind you of your common goal—which is to love the way God loves. Write it down and find someplace where you can put it up and be reminded.

☐ In marriage, you are striving to be on the same page so you make decisions and work well together. But that doesn't mean you have to think exactly the same way all the time. Reflect on a time when you might have approached a situation with different thinking but ultimately found a way to move forward together.

☐ Identify one type of situation or circumstance in which you are prone to forget your common goal. These can be instances when your own needs and agenda might influence your actions more so than remembering to love and accept your partner. Role-play talking to your partner in these situations through the voice of love. What advice would love give them? Switch roles.

YOUR NATURAL ROLES

Each of you should use whatever gift you have
received to serve others, as faithful stewards of
God's grace in its various forms.

1 PETER 4:10

What are things you are naturally good at? It's easy to take your skills and talents for granted, but they are truly a gift from God. Not everyone can do what you find easy to do. Your strengths and abilities are special and valued. And they can be greatly used in your marriage. Each of you should open your minds and intentionally look for how your partner's uniqueness is a benefit, even if it's something you don't fully understand.

My husband and I are different in many significant ways. And early in our marriage, I wasn't confident in some of my areas of strength. I didn't think he appreciated my creativity and fun-natured spirit. I thought I needed to be more serious and disciplined like him. But when I began to really understand just how much intentionality God had in how He created me, I loved those aspects of my personality and saw them as gifts to my husband, our marriage, and our family.

You have been wired a certain way to honor God and advance your marriage in some way. Perhaps you really have the gift of anticipating needs and planning ahead. Or maybe you are a great steward of money. If your partner does not share this gift yet, it's because they don't need to. You are the leader in this area of your marriage. Your leadership with love, grace, understanding, patience, and kindness is all that's needed. Use your gifts to serve each other and not to judge and condemn each other.

REFLECTIONS

- What's something you think your partner is really good at that they may overlook? What are specific examples when they demonstrated this gift? How have you benefited from it? What do you want them to know?

- What are some hidden gifts you have been fearful of sharing? What holds you back? What are you afraid will happen? How long have you been holding on to it? In what ways can your partner support you in sharing your gifts more? How can sharing your gifts make your marriage and life better? How does it honor God?

WORKING TOGETHER THIS WEEK

☐ God has given you gifts to be shared with your partner. Think of something you are good at that you can use to support your spouse. Present it to them as a "present" by writing it down like a coupon they can "cash" in whenever they need your help. Notice how it feels for you to think about your gifts and then intentionally use them to make your marriage relationship even better.

☐ Write your partner a short thank-you note. Express your appreciation for something they have done or said that might not have been a big deal to them but really meant a lot to you. Give this note to them, or hide the note somewhere they will easily find it.

☐ In your prayer time, thank God for how He made each of you. Thank Him for knowing that your partner would need your gifts and that your marriage would be better off when you are using your gifts in ways that glorify Him.

CHOSEN RESPONSIBILITIES

Each one should test their own actions. Then they can take pride in themselves alone, without comparing themselves to someone else, for each one should carry their own load.

GALATIANS 6:4–5

There are times in any marriage when a partner will drop the ball and not be able to do everything they promised to do. This can result in a score-keeping experience where the partner who feels like they are doing everything starts tallying up all the things the other partner is not doing.

Instead of judging if your partner is doing enough, focus on doing what you can. In addition to the natural roles you fulfill in your marriage, there will be chosen responsibilities that you assume. Some of these responsibilities may be a delight for you, and others may truly feel like an obligation. For the latter, it's important to understand both your own internal motivation and the overall benefit of this responsibility being taken care of. There will be times when your partner does not notice or appreciate your contribution and you will need to remind yourself of why you do some of the things you do.

There is a great satisfaction that comes when you are proud of yourself and know that your work on behalf of your family honors God. As you find your rhythm in your family responsibilities, commit to evaluating yourself on a regular basis. Are you executing your tasks to the best of your abilities? Are there things you are leaving for your partner to do but are truly your responsibility? If so, how can you show up better in those areas?

REFLECTIONS

- Are there any responsibilities that are not being taken care of in your marriage or family right now? If so, what are they? What is the plan you'd like to put in place? What's been getting in the way? Why do these responsibilities matter? What are the short-term and long-term benefits to having them assigned and executed?

- What is it like for you when your contributions go unnoticed? How often do you find yourself comparing your set of responsibilities to your partner's? How do you feel in those moments? What would be more productive and helpful to the kind of marriage you want to have together?

WORKING TOGETHER THIS WEEK

☐ This week, find one area of responsibility to switch roles. Intentionally choose something either that you don't love to do or that you know your spouse doesn't love to do. Notice what it's like to lift or take on this burden for a day. Share your experiences with each other.

☐ Next, spend time thinking about how much you appreciate your spouse's effort in this area and express your heartfelt appreciation. Let them know why this matters and the positive impact it has on you and your family.

☐ For any responsibilities not being addressed on a regular basis, brainstorm together your ideas for what to do. Consider if there are other people, besides the two of you, who can help out. What would it be like to ask for help? What concerns come up for you? How might asking for help be a great thing for everyone involved?

SNAPSHOTS IN TIME

For our light and momentary troubles are
achieving for us an eternal glory that far
outweighs them all. So we fix our eyes not on
what is seen, but on what is unseen, since what is
seen is temporary, but what is unseen is eternal.

2 CORINTHIANS 4:17-18

Marriage, like life, is lived in a series of snapshots. You will experience
many seasons, emotions, and experiences together over the course of
your lifetime. Your time together is a journey and not a destination.
There is no "arrival," only the taking of one step after another and
continuing to walk in love. In certain areas, you may make significant
progress, and in others you may feel completely stuck. I want to nor-
malize this for you early on so that you remain committed to getting
through all the stages and phases of being together.

There will be periods of time when you will want your marriage
to be something that it clearly is not. You may want your partner
more focused at home, you may want to spend more time together as
a family, you may want less complaining and more affection. These
times are just snapshots. They do not represent your forever reality.

When you keep your eyes turned above toward God, putting your
faith and hope in Him and what you can't yet see, you will never go
wrong. Any challenges you face are temporary. Any failures you
experience will turn into lessons that will help you move forward.
Having the right perspective makes all the difference. Always stay
focused on what you want the most. The desires God has placed
in your heart are there for a reason: for you to be fulfilled. Don't
become distracted by a reality that's not what God promised you.
Hold on to what you know to be true.

REFLECTIONS

- Reflect on some times in your relationship when things looked one way but then turned in a more positive direction. What was the mindset you adopted in the in-between moments? Were there ways God was speaking to you to let you know all would be well? What did you do to stay focused on the outcome you wanted?

- How can you use the positive moments in your marriage to help you bridge the gap in difficult moments? There will be times when the fun, excitement, and passion may fade. What are your favorite memories together so far? Commit to holding on to them as evidence of things being able to return to being good again.

WORKING TOGETHER THIS WEEK

☐ Go through some of your old photos and select your three favorite memories together. Reminisce about those times and what made them so special for you. What details do you remember? What were you feeling in those moments?

☐ Take a selfie together this week to mark this time of reflection and investment in your marriage. Take turns captioning the photo and share a word of encouragement to the couple in the picture. What do you want them to remember and look back on fondly in the future?

☐ Write a short love note to each other expressing your love and commitment, even in the hard times of marriage. Be sure to include three specific things you want your partner to know or remember during conflict or tension in your relationship.

GROWTH OPPORTUNITIES

Make every effort to add to your faith
goodness; and to goodness, knowledge; and
to knowledge, self-control; and to self-control,
perseverance; and to perseverance, godliness;
and to godliness, mutual affection; and to
mutual affection, love.

2 PETER 1:5–7

This scripture highlights the additive nature of growth. As Believers, the moment you accepted Jesus into your heart a transformation took place. But the inner growth, personal development, and learning do not stop there. In fact, your marriage will be the place of some of your greatest growth and evolution. And the shifts that take place within you may not take place at the same time in your spouse. This is not talked about enough, and many couples believe that they have outgrown each other.

Each of you is on your own journey, and God is shaping you and molding you in just the right way at just the right time. The words of this verse show the progression of growth, but the timeline is infinite and there is no arrival and final destination. There are levels upon levels. When you can recognize this in your marriage, you see all that you experience together as opportunities to grow together.

What will help you grow in love together is being committed to growing in love together. Get in the habit now of learning, being intentional about how you respond and treat each other, operating more like Christ, and treating each other with all the kindness, love, and grace you'd also like to receive. With this mindset, the strength of and fulfillment in your marriage will only grow.

REFLECTIONS

- If you were to truly adopt a mindset of growing together, how might you see various seasons of your marriage differently? What would you spend more time doing when there are challenges between you? What would you spend less time doing in those moments?

- In what ways have you grown personally as a result of being with your partner? How has your relationship shaped you to be more like God? What old habits did you have to let go of? What new habits have you adopted? What's the current growth opportunity that will take your relationship to the next level?

WORKING TOGETHER THIS WEEK

☐ Come up with your own growth plan as a couple. When things feel hard in your marriage, what will you do to make sure you are learning the lessons and growing in the ways you need? How can you build in some accountability? Are there mentors you can turn to for guidance? Consider spiritual leaders, ministries, personal friends, coaches, or counselors.

☐ Think of a challenge you've faced as a couple. How did you grow closer together or deeper in understanding yourself or each other? What is the biggest lesson you learned? Take a minute to celebrate this accomplishment. Give each other a "gold star" by completing this sentence: "I'm so proud that you . . ." Then discuss how what you learned will save you so much time and energy in the future.

☐ There will be times you will notice that your partner could be growing in some ways. Talk together now about one thing you can do to help each other and one thing that you both agree is not helpful at all during those times.

LEADING WITH LOVE

Let love and faithfulness never leave you; bind
them around your neck, write them on the
tablet of your heart.

PROVERBS 3:3

Love. It is what brought you and your partner together. It is a foundational element of sustaining the bond you have. It will help you navigate your differences. It will guide you in understanding each other more. In the day-to-day busyness of life, it's easy to let love for each other take a back seat. You may say things or respond in ways that make it hard to find the love. In these moments, it's important that you develop an awareness and a plan for returning to love.

This scripture offers a vivid description of what it is like to operate from a place of love and faithfulness to each other. When you think of binding something, it doesn't go away. When you think of writing something on your heart, it is permanent. In what ways can you protect the love you feel for each other and lean into it when you are feeling hurt, sad, or frustrated? It is always there to be your guide.

Leading with love means you anchor yourself here. It starts with God, for God *is* love. And He is always with you. Therefore, you always have access to love. It never leaves, even in an argument or disagreement. It's there if you look and listen for it. For your marriage to thrive and flourish, love should be the primary emotion you seek to feel and express together. It is what will ensure your marriage is healthy and growing.

REFLECTIONS

- What does love look like when things are going well in your marriage? How are you treating each other and thinking about each other? What does love look like when things are not going well in your relationship? How do you treat and think about each other then? If in those moments, you were conscious to add just 10 percent more love, what would change?

- What are the ways you intend to keep love at the forefront for you?

WORKING TOGETHER THIS WEEK

☐ Set love reminders by intentionally integrating into your day moments of expressing love to each other. These reminders can be a text message, a handwritten note, a smile, or a hug. The daily habit of living out love will ensure it never leaves your relationship.

☐ Read 1 Corinthians 13:4–8. How is this definition of love playing out in your marriage? What rating would you give yourselves for demonstrating the principles offered in this scripture? What would be one positive shift you can make to operate more out of this definition of love?

☐ Write a love letter to love. Imagine that love is a person. How do you want your relationship to be? How do you want to treat love? How do you want to be treated by love? When do you feel and experience love the most? When does it feel distant and cold? Take this time to get connected to your own personal experiences of love and then share your letter with your partner.

REACHING THE FINISH LINE

And let us run with perseverance the race
marked out for us, fixing our eyes on Jesus, the
pioneer and perfecter of faith.

HEBREWS 12:1–2

In these early days of your marriage, it may be hard to imagine life
30 to 60 years into the future. But you will get there. So many things
about your life will shift and change. So many unexpected things will
happen. The key in reaching the finish line together is keeping your
faith and fixing your mind on Jesus. He is the North Star in all this.

There is a purpose and plan for your union. You are learning
valuable lessons right now that will support you in living out
that plan.

Your commitment and ability to ensure and persevere are the
difference maker. But those are qualities you do not have to generate
on your own. God is the pioneer and perfecter of your faith. He has
already given you the right mindset, skills, and abilities to work well
together as a couple. Your marriage has everything it needs to thrive
in this life and beyond.

As you journey together, you will come across lots of other
examples of marriage and relationships. Social media, television,
movies, songs, and other people in your life will constantly be pro-
viding ideas for what marriage should and should not look like. Your
primary reference point should be God's Word and the insight and
wisdom He gives you both.

REFLECTIONS

- What is the marriage you want to have ten years from now? What do you think you'll have to keep in mind to create that? What things will you need to work on within yourself? How will you need to grow as a couple? What's one thing you could focus on over the next year to position you to reach that goal?

- What would it look like for you to fix your eyes on Jesus in your marriage? How would you operate on a daily basis? How would you handle challenges and uncertainties in your relationship? What things would you start going to Him for that you've been trying to tackle on your own?

WORKING TOGETHER THIS WEEK

☐ What is the finish line you believe God is getting you prepared for as a couple? Write a list of three possible ideas. What signals and signs led you to come up with these ideas? What are your thoughts and feelings? Post your ideas somewhere and revisit them two or three times each year to assess if you're on track or if you feel God leading you in a different direction.

☐ Develop your own motto or statement of perseverance. For example, in my own marriage, we use "Perottes don't stop." What's a statement you can come up with together that's catchy and memorable to help anchor you in the commitment to keep going?

☐ If you were creating a recipe for finishing strong, what would be the ingredients? Come up with ten qualities and characteristics couples need to have in order to endure hardships and keep moving forward to their ultimate goals together.

OUR FAITHFUL JOURNEY

Reflect on the idea of cooperation and what it looks like for you to work well together as a couple. What is your biggest takeaway?

PART 2

BUILDING BETTER COMMUNICATION

Communication is one of those areas in marriage where most couples want to be doing better. Whether your communication is good or bad right now, you'll find a lot of value in the next weeks of this devotional to help you talk to each other in ways that honor the love you want to maintain.

COMMUNICATING WELL TOGETHER

Let your conversation be always full of grace,
seasoned with salt, so that you may know how to
answer everyone.

COLOSSIANS 4:6

Every couple has room to improve their communication. What would it look like for your conversations to be full of grace? Grace in the Christian faith is defined as an unmerited gift of favor. We receive so much from God not because we "deserve" it but because He chooses to be good to us. Consider how it might impact your marriage if you offered your communication as a gift to your partner, even when it seems like they may not deserve it. Let your spirit speak to you on that one. It's powerful.

When your conversation is full of grace, resentment and judgment melt away. The need to be right is of no importance. You'd be less affected by your partner's response to you. You would be careful and intentional with your words. You would use your words to encourage and move you forward together from a place of love. This is what it looks like to truly communicate well. It feels like peace and ease and love. Keep these aspects of communicating in mind as you progress through the next several weeks. It is so much easier to say the right things in the right ways when you view your communication with each other as a gift to your marriage. Communicating well is one important way to take care of your love.

REFLECTIONS

- When you think about God's grace for you, how do you feel? How does knowing that you have unmerited favor influence the way you operate in your life and how you interact with God? Is there any place where you are not experiencing God's grace? How does your ability to recognize His grace toward you affect the grace you are able to show to your partner?

- Reflect on a time when your spouse communicated with you in a way that felt like a gift of grace. What did they say or do that really touched you? How did it impact the way you felt about them and how you felt about yourself?

WORKING TOGETHER THIS WEEK

☐ On a scale from 1 to 10, where 1 is not at all and 10 is all the time, rank how well you think you do communicating with your partner in a way that is gracious and seasoned with salt. Share why you gave the rating you gave. Then identify one thing you could either start or stop doing that would make your communication even better.

☐ Come up with your own definition of what it means for your communication to be full of grace and seasoned with salt. Identify five to ten specific details that represent your definition. Write down this definition on note cards that each of you can display in an area where you'll be regularly reminded of the definition.

☐ Engage in a little loving competition this week for who can be the most gracious in communication, using the definition you came up with. Acknowledge when your partner does a great job of demonstrating the qualities of gracious communication.

DIFFERENT, NOT WRONG

The one who eats everything must not treat with contempt the one who does not, and the one who does not eat everything must not judge the one who does, for God has accepted them.

ROMANS 14:3

You and your partner are different people. The way your brains process information is different. The way you see certain situations is different. The tone you use when communicating is different. The way you prefer to communicate is different. Different—not the same. It does not mean that one way is right and the other is wrong. The more you can adopt this mindset, the better your communication will be.

As a marriage coach, I know a person's ability to use communication skills will vary from situation to situation. Communication in marriage is more about how to work within your differences so you can connect, as opposed to trying to get each other to be perfect.

For communication to work well between the two of you, there should be a measure of acceptance and safety. This scripture reminds us of God's unconditional acceptance of us. Imagine if He were judging our prayers for whether we are using the right skills! We'd second-guess everything and be more hesitant to open up to Him about what's really going on.

When you see your differences as just differences, you release judgment and spend more time trying to understand each other. Talking to each other will feel comfortable and easy. You'll learn to look past any communication differences and really connect with each other's hearts.

REFLECTIONS

- What are some communication differences you have already noticed between you and your partner, and how have you been operating well within those differences? Where can you offer more acceptance and understanding to each other, even if those differences are not your personal preferences?

- God has given you both a set of communication skills that complement each other even though there are times where they seem in conflict. When it's hard to communicate with each other, what would He want you to keep in mind? What lessons might He be trying to teach you so that you can communicate even more effectively?

WORKING TOGETHER THIS WEEK

☐ Identify two communication strengths or skills your partner has. Share with them why you value these skills and how they've served your conversations together. Discuss the things you have learned from your partner about communication and in what ways you recognize your own room for growth.

☐ Describe a time growing up when you felt judged for the way you communicated. Let your partner know what that was like for you and the impact it had on how you talked to other people. Then your partner should write you a brief note or send a short text with words of encouragement for that situation. Once you receive it, reply to your partner with a GIF or emoji that reflects how the gesture made you feel.

☐ In your prayer time with God this week, ask Him to help you experience communication with your partner on a whole new level. Ask for insight and wisdom surrounding any communication differences that make it hard for you to get on the same page and genuinely understand each other.

SUSPENDING JUDGMENT

For in the same way you judge others, you will be
judged, and with the measure you use, it will be
measured to you. Why do you look at the speck of
sawdust in your brother's eye and pay no attention to
the plank in your own eye?

MATTHEW 7:2-3

For the communication in your marriage to work, both of you have
to suspend judgment of each other. This will require your conscious
effort. In our humanness, we are conditioned to categorize, label, and
judge things as either right or wrong, good or bad. In your marriage,
there will be a lot of differences in the way you think and operate.
You will want to talk about these differences as you navigate your
life together with a spirit of curiosity and not judgment.

I remember unpacking boxes with my husband and noticing how
different our approaches were to setting up our home. We had a few
tense debates whether we would keep both pots or just one. We judged
each other—unintentionally—because we were judging the other's
choices against our own.

In marriage especially, the judgment you have toward your
spouse is judgment of yourself. As the scripture reveals, when we
judge others, God will judge us and hold us accountable just the
same. Once you are united in holy matrimony, you become one flesh,
and so as you do unto your spouse, you do unto yourself. Lastly,
many of the judgments we have against our spouse are mere reflections and projections of our own fears, anxieties, and insecurities.

As you notice yourself being tempted to judge, redirect yourself
toward love and understanding. The more you offer acceptance, the
more you will receive it back.

REFLECTIONS

- Judgment is a form of self-righteousness, and part of suspending judgment is being open to the idea that you might be wrong. How easy or hard is this for you to do? Under what circumstances is it easier for you to be more open-minded about a difference between you and your spouse?

- If we are truly judged in the same measure that we judge others, how much judgment should you receive? What do you think causes God to show mercy? What must He think about you? How can you also begin to think those thoughts more about your spouse?

WORKING TOGETHER THIS WEEK

☐ Have an honest conversation together about self-judgment. Identify one area where you often judge yourself. Share why you believe you judge yourself. Discuss how that area is connected to the ways you also judge your spouse. Acknowledge your judgment, and apologize for not being more understanding.

☐ Create a no-judgment zone in your home. Designate a safe space where you both can come to have vulnerable conversations with each other without fear of being judged. Place this scripture in that area, or search the Bible and come up with another helpful reminder to avoid judging each other.

☐ Come up with your own code word that invites you both to suspend judgment and be more understanding of each other during sensitive conversations. Come up with a non-judgment response plan and decide now how you will respond whenever that code word is spoken by either of you.

LEARNING TO LISTEN

My dear brothers and sisters, take note of this:
Everyone should be quick to listen, slow to speak
and slow to become angry.

JAMES 1:19

If there's any skill that is most often missing from communication of any kind between two people, it is the skill of listening. Most people recognize that their listening in a conversation is usually for the purpose of responding. You take information in and then respond. Rarely are we taught to pause, take in what we are hearing, process it fully, and *then* speak. Most times, the quickest thing we do is speak, even before our brains have fully caught up.

Being quick to listen requires that you care as much about what your spouse may want to communicate as you do about what you want to say. When I'm coaching my clients on this, I encourage them to think of what their spouse shares as useful data and necessary information to take them to their next level together as a couple.

When your goal is to listen first, what you say will be more intentional. You'll have better command over your emotions and will be less likely to blow up over something insignificant.

As this week's scripture suggests, we should strive to be slow to anger. When we are truly listening with no assumptions and agenda, this is easier to do. Being slow to anger requires a measure of self-control and intentionality. The Holy Spirit is always there to help you do this when you need.

REFLECTIONS

- Why do you think this advice is so necessary for you in your marriage? Where do you have the hardest time putting this into place? What are you thinking when you have a hard time listening and instead are quick to speak? What would help you slow down?

- How is God a perfect model of this scripture? How does God listen to you? Even though He knows everything about you, He still listens to whatever you bring Him. Why do you think that's the case? How does His ability to listen impact the relationship you have with Him? How could listening more help you in your marriage?

WORKING TOGETHER THIS WEEK

☐ Write down a description of what it looks like when your communication is being well received by your partner. Then discuss a time when you felt like you both demonstrated many of the components of good listening. How did your willingness to listen make the conversation smoother?

☐ Schedule two days of listening sessions this week. During a listening session, one of you has the floor and is able to talk about something that's on your mind without being interrupted. The person listening agrees to practice their listening skills only. Then on another day, they will have the floor, and you will listen to them.

☐ Spend ten minutes together just listening to God. Sit in silence as a couple, invite the Holy Spirit into the room, and listen for the message God has for you. After the time is up, share with each other what you believe you heard.

HAVING CLEAR INTENTIONS

The tongue has the power of life and death, and those who love it will eat its fruit.

PROVERBS 18:21

I can remember a really hard day in my own marriage, years ago, when I blurted out that I didn't think my husband had the capacity to love me the way I wanted to be loved. Those were brutal words I don't think he nor I have ever forgotten. And they weren't true; his love was more than enough. But the words were out there in the space between us, creating more distance.

Our words carry incredible power. They can bring life to what we want, and they can cut us off from what we want. One of the most important things to be clear about is your intentions when you speak to each other. We live so much of our lives unconscious to the actions, words, and energy we bring to our marriages. When you are not careful about how you speak to each other and the goals behind your communication, you are more likely to ramble on and say things that are unhelpful and keep you stuck.

God wants to share His infinite wisdom on this matter. He wants you to test your words and evaluate if they are bringing life or death to your connection as a couple. The old saying "sticks and stones may break my bones, but words will never hurt me" is just not true. Words do hurt. And words can help. It starts with having honorable intentions. You cannot love to talk and prove your point more than you love coming together in unity as a couple.

REFLECTIONS

- Reflect on a time when you said something that was detrimental to your marriage. What led you to say what you said, and how were you feeling? What was the impact of your words on your spouse? What do you want them to know now?

- We've all been a part of conversations that seemed pointless at the time, both within and outside our marriage. What are the things that make a conversation feel unproductive or unhelpful to you? What's something that's worked for you in the past to turn a pointless conversation into a productive and meaningful one?

WORKING TOGETHER THIS WEEK

☐ Come up with three different kinds of intentions you might have for a conversation (such as expressing appreciation, raising a concern, and making a request). What are some words or phrases you can use to be clear at the beginning what your goal is for the discussion? How can you also invite God in to help you craft the intention behind it?

☐ Speak life into your marriage right now by making a declaration. What is something you want to speak into existence for yourselves as a couple? Find a scripture that supports this declaration. Then identify one step you can take this week that will move you closer to that reality.

☐ As a couple, identify someone in your life you'd like to encourage. Pray for them now and use your words to intercede on their behalf. If you feel it's appropriate, send them a note or text to let them know you are praying for them. How does coming together in this way benefit your own communication?

THE POWERFUL PAUSE

The heart of the righteous weighs its answers, but
the mouth of the wicked gushes evil.

PROVERBS 15:28

My husband is a master of slow, careful communication when
we speak. I marvel at how much time he takes to think before he
says something. It is a skill I think all of us should have more of. At
first, I did not think this. He would take minutes to respond to me
sometimes. But I discovered that the quiet spaces in between my sen-
tences to him were just deliberate pauses so that he could carefully
choose his words.

What about you? When you think about pausing and taking your
sensitive conversations more slowly, what comes up? One of the
most challenging things about communicating well in a marriage is
allowing yourself to create new rules that work for you. We get into
habits and socially conditioned ways of being in intimate relationships. The care and intention you give when talking to a supervisor
at work are probably much different from the way you speak to your
spouse. Why? What is the reason you might choose to be more careful in a professional setting and less careful at home?

God's wisdom here is so valuable. If there is one powerful step
you can take to improve your communication, it is pausing before
you respond. This act, which may only take ten seconds, can mean
the difference between a conversation that helps and heals any
issues and one that hurts and hinders progress on any issues. It's
always worth the time to slow yourself down and let the inner
wisdom of the Holy Spirit and the higher-thinking part of your brain
take the lead.

REFLECTIONS

- Which one of you is more careful and takes time to intentionally choose how you communicate to the other? How did you develop this skill? What are the thoughts that help you take this action? How can you be a loving leader in this area and support your spouse in doing the same?

- Describe a time when you were not careful with your words. What did you say that you later regretted? What was the impact on the other person? How did you feel about yourself? What do you wish you had done differently? How do those lessons impact your approach to communicating in your marriage now?

WORKING TOGETHER THIS WEEK

☐ Practice pausing for ten seconds as much as possible this week when you are engaged in conversation. I recommend doing this in any kind of conversation—not just contentious ones. Practicing this skill when you are not upset will make it that much easier when conversations get a little tense.

☐ Set aside time to pray for each other in this area. Invite God into your challenging conversations. As you pray, practice being careful and deliberate with your words. Notice whether this feels comfortable or difficult for you to practice. After you pray, discuss the experience. Share what it was like for you to pray and to be prayed for.

☐ Express gratitude and appreciation to each other for the ways in which you are already careful in your communication. Describe a time when your partner said something that let you know they cared or a time when you felt really special because of their words to you.

HEART SEARCH

Search me, God, and know my heart; test me and
know my anxious thoughts. See if there is any
offensive way in me, and lead me in the
way everlasting.

PSALM 139:23-24

Knowing what you are feeling and why is the skill of self-awareness.
You want to always be conscious of how your emotions are directing
your actions—especially how you communicate with each other.
This is an area where God wants to help you if you invite Him in. As
David shows us in his example, we should go to God requesting He
show us our own heart and what's inside.

In marriage, there are often many emotions that create conflict—
fear, anxiety, anger, disappointment, frustration, guilt, shame,
inadequacy, rejection, resentment. When we feel these emotions in
our heart and don't know what to do with them, we may lash out or
shut down in a conversation. When you invite God in to search your
heart and show you how you are thinking and what you are feeling,
you have supernatural insight into yourself. This inner knowing will
help you know what to say and what not to say. It will help you know
when to pause a conversation and take care of your emotions on
your own or with God before bringing something to your spouse.

Even in my own marriage, I'm aware of how much the emotion
of rejection comes up for me. I've learned to notice how it feels in my
body and to appropriately attribute that feeling to specific thoughts
instead of blaming my husband and making him the reason I feel a
certain way. As you develop this skill, God is your partner.

REFLECTIONS

- What stood out to you the most from this day's reading? Had you ever considered how your emotions affect the way you communicate? Do you now see anything about yourself or your spouse differently? What might change if you start sharing more about how you're feeling with each other? How might you find this difficult?

- If God were to search your heart on a regular basis, what would He find? What message might he have for you that would help you communicate better? What word of encouragement might he have for you as you navigate some challenging emotions?

WORKING TOGETHER THIS WEEK

☐ On a scale of 1 to 10, where 1 is not at all and 10 is a great deal, how self-aware are you? How conscious are you to how you are feeling in a given moment and how your feelings affect your actions? This week, take extra care to ask yourself each day, how am I feeling right now? Then notice the specific thoughts that you are thinking and are associated with the feeling that comes up for you. Share what you learn with your spouse.

☐ Look back over the ten emotions listed in the commentary. Write down the ones most often in your heart when you have conflict. Discuss together how your emotions are similar or different. Describe how you typically respond to these emotions. How can you both support each other in dealing with these emotions?

MAKE NO ASSUMPTIONS

To answer before listening—that is folly and shame.

PROVERBS 18:13

Our human brains are always making meaning of situations. We like to understand things by making assumptions. These assumptions can be based on previous experiences or may just be a result of our own preconceived notions. In marriage, the more you assume things first, the greater the chance you are going to have misunderstandings, hurt feelings, and frustrating experiences with each other. Keeping this proverb in mind will lend some valuable guidance to you as you work to make your communication the best it can be.

It's easier to avoid making assumptions when you pause and train yourself to ask questions of each other rather than making statements *at* each other. And it's easier to pause when you are not extremely emotionally charged. When I'm coaching my clients, I teach them how to assess their emotional reactivity—how emotional they are currently feeling about the topic of conversation. When you are emotionally reactive, you are more likely to spout off before listening to the facts. Being in tune with your emotions and noticing how you feel physically when you are emotionally charged are helpful during difficult conversations.

This may be hard sometimes. But if God instructs us to do something, He also gives us the power and ability to carry it through. What do you both gain when you avoid making assumptions and truly seek to understand each other? Most people find that when they are impatient in their communication, they feel guilty afterward. In a calmer state, they recognize how they could have done things differently. This is important, too. We will not get things perfect all the time.

REFLECTIONS

• At what times and in which situations are you more likely to answer before listening to the facts? Why do you think these circumstances are so impactful to you? What fear do they bring up? How can you speak more vulnerably in these moments and see the situation from a calmer and more open place?

• Describe a time when you wanted to get really angry and make assumptions but were able to keep your calm. What was the situation? What helped you do that? What did you learn in that conversation that otherwise you would not have known?

WORKING TOGETHER THIS WEEK

☐ Together, come up with a question or phrase that can help you both remember to listen before answering in potentially tense conversations. Consider how you can make it fun, light-hearted, and playful for you both.

☐ Practice your listening skills by instructing your spouse to complete a simple task (such as folding a shirt, drawing an object, or doing an exercise move). Give them verbal directions that they are to follow without asking questions. Then switch roles. Reflect on any assumptions you made and what it was like to just listen.

☐ Read the rest of Proverbs 18 and identify any other verses that you find helpful in making your communication better. For any verse you pick out, describe what you find most helpful and how applying the idea behind it will be beneficial to you.

TIMING IS EVERYTHING

> There is a time for everything, and a season for
> every activity under the heavens: [...] a time to be
> silent and a time to speak.
>
> ECCLESIASTES 3:1, 7

Holding your tongue when you really want to say something can be one of the hardest things to do. It's like there is a little switch inside your head that keeps coming on and lighting you up. The urge to make a comment, ask a question, or get the last word is strong. But there are times when it's completely unnecessary and can actually damage a relationship.

If you struggle with this, it's important to understand why. Much of our impatience to talk comes from valuing our perspective more than that of the other person. We think our way is right or that what we have to say is the most important thing in the moment. There will be times when this is true and also times when it is not.

God is the only one who truly knows exactly when we should speak and when we should hold off. He is available to help you know what to do. Whenever I'm trying to discern the will of God in a situation, big or small, I think about what I know about Him and His word. God is always concerned with the welfare of both you and your spouse. He would never want you to say something at a time that is not right for the both of you. When you see the way you communicate with your spouse as a gift, then you will want to make sure your timing is good.

REFLECTIONS

- Even the right thing said at the wrong time can be unhelpful. Think of a time when this happened for you—either you had the wrong timing or someone speaking to you did so at an inappropriate time. What was that like? What made the timing poor? How would things have gone differently if the timing had been better?

- Sometimes in the moments when you are not speaking, God has an opportunity to work and reveal something to you or your spouse. Think of a time when this was true—when you refrained from saying something and God worked it out anyway.

WORKING TOGETHER THIS WEEK

☐ Reflect on when the timing of a conversation might not have been the best. What signals do you give when you are not prepared to have a conversation? How do you want to handle these situations moving forward? If either of you approaches a conversation at an undesirable time, how can you kindly let the other person know?

☐ Decide if you'd like to have a regularly scheduled check-in time together on either a weekly or monthly basis. If you do, discuss what you want to accomplish in this check-in time. It can be for the goal of connecting, discussing any issues, or planning for your future.

☐ Identify three obstacles that prevent you from holding your tongue when doing so is necessary. Take each one of these obstacles to God in prayer this week, and ask Him to give you the wisdom, discipline, or insight to work through them effectively.

YOUR ENERGY MATTERS

In the same way, let your light shine before others,
that they may see your good deeds and glorify your
Father in heaven.

MATTHEW 5:16

The energy you bring to a situation and conversation matters.
Usually, when we are upset or unhappy, our energy reflects this state.
We go to our spouse frustrated, and our tone is sometimes unkind.
Usually, our spouse, in their own humanness, responds the same
way. It's natural to think that voicing complaints and expressing
our displeasure will lead to change. But I have found the opposite is
true, and, in fact, when we approach situations with love, we create a
lasting change.

We've all heard the quote often attributed to Mahatma Gandhi,
"Be the change you want to see in the world." That is also true in
marriage. So much more positive change comes about when you let
your light of love, kindness, compassion, and understanding shine.
The best example of this is our relationship with God Himself. When
we think about His goodness and His unconditional love and acceptance, we can't help but want to do better. He models the standard of
excellence that we then strive to meet.

How you communicate and show up in your marriage can be
a wonderful form of worship unto the Lord. You can glorify Him
in how you treat and speak to your partner. When your energy
represents the essence of God and love, your conversations go so
much better. Letting your light shine will look different in different
moments and circumstances. But just the thought alone can elevate
your attitude and the energy you bring to your spouse.

REFLECTIONS

- What does it mean to let your light shine? How would others describe you when your light is shining bright and glorifying God? How do you feel when you are letting your light shine? What's different about you in these instances?

- Describe a time when you brought the energy of light to a situation that felt dark. This can be a conversation with someone in a bad or sad mood or a situation that was going wrong and you brought positivity and hope. How did the other people respond? What made you show up so positively?

WORKING TOGETHER THIS WEEK

☐ Light a candle together while sitting in a dark room. Spend a few minutes just watching the flame and keep this verse in mind. What comes up for you? What do you notice about the light in the dark room? How does it change things? How can you, letting your light shine, change things, too?

☐ Let your spouse know of a time when you felt like they let their light shine and demonstrated the love of God. This can be a big moment or small moment in your life together. Discuss why you noticed this and the impact it had on you personally.

☐ Come up with a good deed you'd like to do together as a couple this week. It can be anything and benefit anyone in your life. After you decide what you will do, reflect on this idea. In what ways does this deed represent who you want to be as a couple?

KNOWING WHAT YOU WANT

You do not have because you do not ask God.
When you ask, you do not receive, because you ask
with wrong motives, that you may spend what you
get on your pleasures.

JAMES 4:2–3

One of the greatest communication skills you can have in your marriage is expressing what you want. I was recently coaching a newly married couple who had an infant. The wife wanted her husband to help out more and was often frustrated that all the childcare responsibilities fell on her. When I asked her exactly what she wanted her husband to do, she didn't have a specific answer. During our session together, we worked through a process to help her get extremely specific about what he could do that would be helpful to her. She presented this to him, and he eagerly agreed. He appreciated her specificity and was happy to finally feel like he was doing things right in her eyes.

In your own marriage, there will be plenty of times you want your spouse to do something but only communicate in a vague way. I highly recommend you get in the habit of being specific about what you'd like—making a tangible request to which they can reply "yes," "no," or "not right now." This helps you get on the same page and avoid the frustration of not having easy expectations and needs met.

God has instructed us on how to pray and ask Him for things. He wants us to be clear and to also have the right motives. As you think about your motives in making requests of your spouse, be sure they honor both of you, God, and your marriage.

REFLECTION

- If you can be very honest, when have you made requests and had motives that were self-serving instead of God-serving? How did you know your intentions were not the best? What happened with your request—did it come to pass or not? How did you feel as a result? What did you think?

WORKING TOGETHER THIS WEEK

☐ Create a checklist together of positive intentions. For example, what are good reasons to make requests, discuss any challenges, and have hard conversations together? Get in the habit of stating your positive intentions when you initiate conversations with each other.

☐ Think of a specific request you'd like to ask your spouse. First, assess your intentions and determine whether this request honors both of you. Spend some time taking this desire to God and asking Him to give you insight and wisdom. If you find that your request is coming from the right place, prepare yourself to talk to your partner. If you find it's not, then ask God to show you what He wants for you instead.

☐ Then, as appropriate, make your request, being as specific as possible. Invite your spouse to ask clarifying questions so they understand specifically what you are asking. Allow them to honestly say yes or no to your request without pressure from you.

FOCUS ON SOLUTIONS

Trust in the Lord with all your heart and lean not on
your own understanding; in all your ways submit to
him, and he will make your paths straight.

PROVERBS 3:5–6

As you and your spouse solve problems together, you have a faithful
guide in the Lord. He wants to lead you and guide you in working
through your differences and resolving any conflict. There is a solution to any challenge you will face as a couple. This may not always
be clear to you, but it's clear to God. He will send the Holy Spirit to
show you the way when you invite Him to do so. This often requires
patience beyond what may be comfortable. Consider the ways you
can partner together as you wait for and receive God's direction and
guidance.

There will be times in your marriage when you have conversations and lose sight of finding solutions. You both may be so upset
or otherwise focused on your feelings that the priority of solving
your issues takes a back seat. This is what commonly happens when
people vent. They lose sight of trying to move forward and spend too
much time on the problem.

As you and your spouse navigate communication, you'll want to
balance the honest expression of your needs and feelings with an
eye toward progressing forward. Focusing on solutions will enable
you to keep the big picture in mind, and you'll be less distracted by
details that are less relevant to the goals that matter the most.

REFLECTIONS

- What does it look like for you to trust in the Lord and not lean on your own understanding? How easy or hard is it for you to do so? Why is this the case? When are the times it's easiest? When is it hardest for you? What would make it easier?

- Discuss a time in your relationship when you were grateful to be able to lean on God's wisdom. What was the situation? How did your relationship with God help you? What would have been different if you had relied only on your own knowledge and wisdom?

WORKING TOGETHER THIS WEEK

☐ Start each day this week inviting the Holy Spirit to give you a new level of wisdom and understanding in your day-to-day activities. Make a note of this request and put it somewhere so you can remember. At the end of the week, discuss how this worked for you.

☐ Identify one way you can begin to acknowledge God more in your life. How might doing this lead you to achieve more success and fulfillment in your efforts? Why does it matter to you to acknowledge God? Are there certain situations where this is harder? Why? How can your spouse support you?

☐ What's something you've been trying to do on your own as a couple? What would it look like for you to turn that situation completely over to God? What concerns would you have? And conversely, how might this offer you greater peace? What is one step you can take today to put it in God's hands?

SPEAKING THE
TRUTH IN LOVE

Instead, speaking the truth in love, we will grow to
become in every respect the mature body of him
who is the head, that is, Christ.

EPHESIANS 4:15

Speaking the truth in love is a popular idea from the Bible. Yet, like
so many things we've covered together, the application requires
intentional thought and practice. I want to leave you with the idea
that your communication with each other will sometimes feel
like experimenting. The goal is not to be perfect in every single
encounter but to constantly look at ways to apply these principles
so you can be effective together. There will be days you may try
to speak the truth in love and it goes over well. Other days, it may
go horribly wrong. Keep going. Keep trying. Keep deepening your
understanding.

Just as you are aiming to be gracious in communicating with
your spouse, you should also be gracious to yourself. As a newly
married couple, you are constantly learning what works and
what doesn't work for you both. You are growing and maturing
together. You are stretching yourself to be and walk more like God
every day. That's why you are here reading this devotional.

Consider the goal of speaking the truth in love as a journey. As
you learn more about God and His ways, you'll get better and better
at it. As you learn more about yourself and each other, you'll get
better and better at it. Love is a principle that stands the test of time.
Even if a conversation goes wrong, you can always find a way to
return to love—for God, yourself, and your spouse.

REFLECTIONS

- How can speaking the truth in love bring you and your spouse closer together? What elements of speaking from a place of love need to be present in order for that to happen? How will you be able to know when you are doing that effectively or when some improvement is still necessary?

- What does it mean to you to grow in the maturity of Christ? What qualities would you embody more of? What would you do less of? How often do you find yourself assessing your thoughts and actions against the model that is Jesus?

WORKING TOGETHER THIS WEEK

☐ Using the word "love," come up with your own acronym or acrostic poem for what it means for you both to speak the truth in love to each other. Write this down and post it somewhere as a reminder.

☐ You can also speak the truth in love for positive things in your marriage. This week, share a loving appreciation to your spouse. Offer something you know to be true about them and how valuable that quality is to your marriage, now and into the future.

☐ On a scale from 1 to 10, where 1 is very hard and 10 is not hard at all, how easy is it for you to speak the truth of how you feel and what you want? What do you think influences you the most on this? What did you learn about expressing yourself as a child? How is it showing up in your marriage now? Identify any changes you'd like to make that would be helpful.

OUR FAITHFUL JOURNEY

Read Ephesians 4:29–32. In what ways does this passage summarize many of the concepts we've discussed in this part of the devotional?

_____

_____

_____

_____

_____

_____

_____

_____

_____

_____

_____

_____

_____

_____

_____

_____

RESOLVING CONFLICT WITH GRACE

There will be many points of conflict over the life of your marriage. In part 3, you will receive tools and perspectives to help you navigate these times in a way that enhances and doesn't hurt your marriage. In fact, conflict, when handled well, can actually bring you closer.

RULES OF ENGAGEMENT

Therefore confess your sins to each other and
pray for each other so that you may be healed.
The prayer of a righteous person is powerful
and effective.

JAMES 5:16

When couples are in conflict, two perspectives are at play. Most times, conflict arises when each person is determined to prove their point at the expense of their spouse's perspective. They see things their way and believe they are right. But if you want to resolve conflict in healthy and honorable ways, you both should be honest with yourselves and each other. This means looking at where you may be seeing things incorrectly or being open to a perspective different from your own.

When I'm working with couples in my practice, I often suggest they create rules of engagement when they are having sensitive discussions in which disagreements might arise. They come up with a list of dos and don'ts—things that are acceptable, things that are not. This verse provides a wonderful example of what some rules of engagement might look like for you and your spouse. How would your conversations go if this was the standard to which you both held yourselves?

Whenever you are in intense conflict, something is surfacing that's unhealed in each of you. Sometimes you may not even be aware of it. But just like a body gets a fever when it encounters an infection, so, too, will your discussions get very heated when there is something going on within you. God knows and God can heal what needs to be healed. As a couple, make it a rule to pray for each other's healing. Even if your initial motivation is so that you can have calm and peaceful conversations, it's something you want to get in the habit of doing.

REFLECTIONS

- What makes it easy to confess your sins to each other, and how often do you find yourself doing this? What are the things that stand in your way? Has there been a time when you did confess some shortcoming and afterward felt that it hadn't been emotionally safe to do so? What had you needed from your spouse at that time?

- What do you think of your spouse when they are able to vulnerably confess their sin or weakness to you? How does it impact your connection? In what ways does that help you resolve your conflict productively?

WORKING TOGETHER THIS WEEK

☐ Together, come up with your own rules of engagement list for discussing sensitive topics. What are the things you will do and the things you agree not to do? Why do these things matter to you both? How will you support each other in being accountable for these agreements?

☐ Share with each other something you believe God is healing or has healed you from physically, emotionally, or otherwise. What was your life like before? How is your life different now? Say a quick prayer of gratitude for that healing.

☐ Rate the effectiveness of your prayer on a scale from 1 to 10 (1 being not at all, 10 being very much). Why did you give it this rating? What's one thing that you think would make your prayer more effective? Are you comfortable receiving help in this area? Why or why not?

DISAGREEMENTS, NOT INDICTMENTS

Settle matters quickly with your adversary
who is taking you to court. Do it while you are
still together on the way, or your adversary
may hand you over to the judge, and the judge
may hand you over to the officer, and you may
be thrown into prison.

MATTHEW 5:25

It is normal—even healthy—for couples to have disagreements. No one is perfect, and your spouse will say things or do things that you don't agree with or that you think are completely wrong. It's important that you separate your disapproval of their *behavior* from your disapproval of them as a *person*. Many times, couples get into trouble when they take a mistake or bad decision and then become the judge and jury about their spouse's character.

This verse reminds us that you want to discuss, address, and settle disagreements quickly, while you are still thinking positively about each other overall. Once resentment and long-held negative beliefs about each other take over, it's like you imprison your spouse in your mind. You view everything about them from an adversarial perspective. You become unable to give them the benefit of the doubt and a huge wedge forms between you.

Settling matters quickly means you don't let things fester. You keep your goal of a healthy, loving connection as a top priority. When you truly see and believe you can figure things out together, there is no need to delay or avoid having tough conversations. You see them as opportunities to bring you closer.

REFLECTIONS

* Are there times you have made your spouse's choices mean something bigger about who they are as a person? For example, if they make the choice to work late, do you tell yourself that they are selfish and inconsiderate of your family's needs? After reading this scripture and commentary, what have you learned?

* The scripture instructs settling matters "while you are still on your way." What does that mean to you in your marriage? Do you feel like your relationship is in this place right now? Why or why not? What would help get you or keep you there?

WORKING TOGETHER THIS WEEK

☐ Spend time this week creating a list of "no matter what" thoughts. These are thoughts you will always choose to think about each other, even when you do not like or agree with your spouse's decisions or choices.

☐ Discuss together what it will look like for you to settle matters quickly in your marriage. If you have different definitions, how can you still come together in a way that works for both of you? When are times you have not settled things quickly? What was the impact? What will help keep you on track?

☐ Pray together that God would help you both see each other as He sees you. What is God trying to convey to you? How can you be intentional about seeing your spouse the way God does? Throughout the week, pay special attention to the judgments you form about each other, and bring those thoughts to God.

BEYOND THE TRIGGER

Search me, God, and know my heart; test me
and know my anxious thoughts. See if there
is any offensive way in me, and lead me in the
way everlasting.

PSALM 139:23-24

I once worked with a couple who had a heated argument about bagged salad. The concern of one person was that the salad was going to waste and the money was used unwisely. The other person didn't think it was a big deal and wanted their spouse to see it the same way. The argument escalated into a big fight. They are not the first (or probably the last) people who have had this exact argument.

What I told these clients is that the argument is never about the specific thing you are arguing about. A deeper fear or worry is always underneath it, causing you to feverishly fight for your position. It's the difference between a surface issue and a root issue. In this case, the root issue was fear and scarcity around money, not because they were in financial hardship, but mostly because it was an ingrained belief passed down during childhood.

All of us have foundational belief systems that cause us to be extra sensitive to certain circumstances. For this conversation, I'll call those "triggers": the things that set you off and take you from zero to 100 rather quickly. Whenever you notice yourself over-reacting to something, it's a signal to find out what your overreaction is really about. What are you really reacting to? Is it really a problem that your spouse doesn't help out enough around the house, or might it be that you feel uncomfortable asking for help, so you do every-thing on your own? Being able to identify what is really underneath the initial trigger will help you focus on solving the right problem.

REFLECTIONS

- What stood out to you about this verse, the commentary, and the notion of anxious thoughts? What anxious thoughts might you have? How do they come into play during conflict with each other? How can God help you with your thoughts?

- What are your thoughts about root issues versus surface issues? Is this a perspective you had previously considered? How do you see this idea playing out in your marriage? Do you find that as a couple you are trying to solve for surface issues or root issues? What does it look like to do one versus the other?

WORKING TOGETHER THIS WEEK

☐ Discuss together two common triggers you react to—both within and outside your marriage. Each consider the following questions and then take turns sharing answers: What are the physical and emotional responses that let you know you're being triggered? What do you feel in your body? What do you do? What makes these triggering situations so problematic for you? When did you first notice you had such a strong reaction to this thing? Why do you think that is?

☐ Identify an issue in your marriage that brings up conflict. If you assume the conflict is really *not* about the specific issue, what else could it be about? Come up with three alternative root causes to this issue. How would you approach solving each of these root issues?

☐ Pray with your partner, asking God to lead you both through your root issues. He wants to guide you and help you work through the root issues. What would it take for you to trust Him more with the things that trigger you? What's one thing you will try this week?

WHAT'S GOING ON INSIDE

What causes fights and quarrels among you?
Don't they come from your desires that battle
within you?

JAMES 4:1

One of the greatest lessons I've learned is that marriage is one of the best pathways to learning more about yourself. Every day, in some small way, there is an opportunity to search and better understand yourself. When you are in conflict with each other, you are also in conflict with yourself. Something is agitating you, frustrating you, and causing you to be upset. Most people attribute that to what their spouse is doing. But I want you to learn it's the best time to look at yourself.

The skill of self-reflection is one of the most powerful, yet least developed, skills in most relationships. We are not taught how to understand what we are thinking and feeling. Yet our thoughts and feelings are the drivers of our behaviors, so if you are arguing with your spouse, it's because of *your* thoughts and feelings. Their action or speech is the occasion for your thought and emotion. Once you understand what you are thinking and feeling, you can make decisions and respond in ways that help you and your marriage grow.

This scripture talks about the battle within you, which creates battles among you. What's going on inside you when you are in conflict? What old fears, worries, and concerns are being bumped up against? What childhood wound is being exposed? When you sit and allow yourself to understand why you are reacting the way you are, God can help heal you. This will make many of your moments of conflict irrelevant, and they will be nonissues for you moving forward.

REFLECTIONS

- How familiar are you with the concept of self-awareness? When did you first learn about it? What examples from the Bible can you think of where self-awareness was demonstrated? What do you think God's role is in self-awareness?

- What are some of the ways you battle within yourself? What things do you worry about, do you feel guilty about, or are you hard on yourself about? How does that internal battle sometimes spill over into your marriage? What would you like to happen instead? How can your spouse help you?

WORKING TOGETHER THIS WEEK

☐ This week, pay close attention to what you are thinking and feeling in challenging situations. Write down your thoughts and how you react (on your phone or in a journal). Then come together and share what you noticed. Now, with more self-awareness, is there anything you would change about how you reacted? Why or why not?

☐ Where do you think your desires differ from your spouse's? Where do you both want the same things? Which list do you think about more? For the next week, focus only on the desires you share. Look for examples of where this is true and point them out to each other. Notice how finding the similarities makes it easier to deal with the differences.

☐ What's one thing you wish you didn't have conflict about? What would it take from you in order for you to be more on the same page? How can you take full responsibility for your part in this being an issue for you as a couple?

RIGHT AND WRONG

There is a way that appears to be right, but in
the end it leads to death.

PROVERBS 14:12

When you know better, you do better ... sometimes. Many of us
know the right thing to do in certain situations. Yet for some reason
we find ourselves making choices or taking actions that don't represent what we'd say is right. In an effort to protect our egos, we justify
our decisions and make excuses. People can sometimes fall into the
trap of making wrong decisions right just by the way they choose
to see them. The human brain is exceptional at finding evidence for
what you want it to believe.

I see this happen a lot with couples who are in conflict. One
spouse has built up a case for their actions, and even though it goes
against what their partner believes is right, they still fight for their
position. It feels vulnerable to admit any wrongdoing, and many
times pride and ego stand in the way of seeing right from wrong.
Ultimately, this results in a spouse becoming more bothered by their
partner's unwillingness or inability to take responsibility than what
actually occurred.

This scripture is a helpful reminder of how we don't always have
the clear picture. What we think is right now could be very wrong
tomorrow. While many of the day-to-day decisions you'll make in
your marriage are unlikely to lead to physical death, they may lead
to a death in your connection to and image of each other. Leaning
on God's guidance is so critical. Be in the habit of submitting your
desires, ideas, and actions to Him.

REFLECTIONS

- Think back to a time when you convinced yourself you were making a good decision, only to find out it was a bad choice. What made you think it was the right thing to do? What did you come to see later? Knowing what you know now, what would you have told yourself? Do you think you would have listened to your own advice?

- Discuss a time when someone you cared about made a decision you could see was wrong, but they had convinced themselves it was right. What was it like for you to watch them make a poor choice? Did you share your thoughts? If so, how did you do it? What was their response?

WORKING TOGETHER THIS WEEK

☐ How will you decide upon what's considered right and wrong in your marriage? What are the standards you want to agree to uphold? How can you invite God into your conversation as you make these decisions together?

☐ How would you like to handle moments in your marriage in which one person thinks something is right and the other person thinks it is wrong? What's the best way to approach each other? What will you do if they are not open to your feedback? What boundaries could you set to ensure you are taking care of yourself?

☐ Spend a few minutes sharing a time when you saw your spouse do something that you felt was really right and honorable. What were you thinking about them when they took action that aligned with what you considered right? Did you let them know at the time? Why or why not? What is it like to share this with them now?

COOLING OFF

Better a patient person than a warrior, one
with self-control than one who takes a city.

PROVERBS 16:32

Points of disagreement don't have to turn into heated arguments
when you are able to manage your emotions well. There will be
times of conflict when the best next step is to take some time to cool
off rather than push the issue. One way to know this is how urgent it
feels for you to talk. Whenever you are emotionally charged, it will
feel urgent for you to talk to your spouse, get them to see your point,
and ultimately get them to agree with you. This is never the ideal
time to resolve your conflict. Instead, take time to cool off.

This scripture reminds us of the value of patience. Practicing
patience means you feel the urge to do something now, but you see
the benefit of waiting. You essentially override the urge and allow
more sound judgment and reason to take over. God has given us all
the power of self-control. Often, we are more persuasive and influen-
tial with gentleness than aggressive and combative communication.
In the moment, this is hard to see. What I think most people do recognize is when they are feeling intense emotions. In these moments,
just ask God to give you strength to restrain yourself. He will do it.

If you find yourself really struggling to cool off in the moment,
consider this a work in progress for yourself. When you blow up or
lose your temper, take the time to reflect on what happened for you.
Sometimes the hindsight learning will be even more valuable than
if you had de-escalated the argument in the moment. Being able to
identify what you were thinking and feeling will help you understand how to navigate similar interactions in the future.

REFLECTIONS

- Reflect on a time when you needed to cool off. What was happening, and what signals suggested that you needed to cool off? What did you do in response, and was it effective? Contrast that with a time when you needed to cool off but didn't. What was the difference in those conversations?

- What is it like to be in a discussion with someone who needs to cool off? How do you typically respond? Describe a time when that approach worked and when it didn't. How did you feel in each instance? What were your thoughts about the other person? Did the situation have any long-term impact on your relationship?

WORKING TOGETHER THIS WEEK

☐ What are some ways you find are helpful for you when you need to cool off? What are the things that do not work for you? How do you know when you are cooled off? What do you feel in your body? How do you approach conversations from a grounded, calm place? If this remains a challenge, can you reach out to a pastor, counselor, or coach for more guidance?

☐ Some couples find it helpful to create a code word to signal that someone needs to cool off (page 37). If you were to come up with your own code word, what would it be? How easy or hard would it be for you to cool off if your partner said the code word to you during a conversation?

☐ If you could imagine God having a cool-off plan, what would it be? Given what you know of His character, how would He think about it? In what ways can you lean on His wisdom and guidance when you need to cool off?

WHAT THE MARRIAGE NEEDS

Anyone who does not provide for their relatives,
and especially for their own household, has
denied the faith and is worse than an unbeliever.

1 TIMOTHY 5:8

One of the most valuable perspectives I want to offer you is the idea that your marriage is a living, breathing being that needs your time, care, and effort. I often like to think of it as a newborn baby. Imagine it being helpless, unable to grow or thrive unless you are attentive and responsive to its needs. When you and your spouse are in conflict, you cannot give your marriage what it needs, and it is harmed.

Your marriage has to come first in order for it to be what it can be. If there are points when it feels like it's limping along, you have to ask, "What's missing here?" You'll find there is less room for conflict and disagreement. Instead, you will want to work through things quickly so that your marriage can continue to flourish. The more you focus on what's good for your marriage, the less focused you will be on your own preferences, offenses, and frustrations.

This verse is a potent reminder of how dedicated we should be to the health and well-being of our own households. It's something we are called to do. It's an act of love for God, and as Believers in the faith, what you do for your marriage will always be rewarded by God. Consider that He has given you your marriage as a sacred gift and has charged you with taking care of it. Where does conflict among you fit in with taking good care of your marriage? My prayer is that you will find it doesn't and that you will be quick to compromise and resolve your differences.

REFLECTIONS

- What do you think of the idea of your marriage being a newborn baby? What would be different for you if you adopted this thinking? What would you do more or less of in order to take the best care of it?

- Are there any places where you feel like you've missed the mark on nurturing your marriage the way you should? What needs might you have neglected? How can you see those gaps in a loving and compassionate way while you work to now give your marriage what it needs?

WORKING TOGETHER THIS WEEK

☐ This week, work together to give your marriage a persona. Consider giving it a name and treating it like a baby. Decide how you want the "baby" to grow and what you will do so that you both take good care of it. What are the conflicts you are committed to resolving out of love and care for your marriage?

☐ Write down a list of things your marriage needs. Even in your differences, consider how each of you is uniquely created to take care of all the needs together. With this perspective, what do you think about conflict? How can you begin to use your differences to take better care of your marriage?

☐ Think about an argument or point of conflict you had recently. What was it about? What were you thinking that made things a problem? In your conflict, what message did you communicate to your marriage? What it a positive message or a harmful message? What do you want your marriage to know now?

MEETING IN THE MIDDLE

> If it is possible, as far as it depends on you, live
> at peace with everyone.
>
> **ROMANS 12:18**

What if I told you there was always a way to work through any conflict in your marriage? The only perspective you need to adopt is that of meeting in the middle. Conflict exists only when two people refuse to budge on their position. If you want to work out any issue, you will work out the issue. It's important that you tell yourself the truth on this. Issues don't get resolved when one or both of you are more committed to your position than being committed to finding a mutually workable solution.

When you make living in peace your primary goal, you are more open to finding ways to compromise. Rarely in life are there things that are absolutely black and white. There is always some gray area that can be created. But in order for you to see that as a couple, you should first commit to meeting in the middle.

This does not mean you have to agree on everything all the time. But it does mean you seek to find ways in which the desires and needs of both people are recognized and honored in some way. Think about this: Meeting in the middle overall feels better than convincing or demanding your spouse to get on board with your way. When you step back, you have to ask, "Do I want to be a person who makes my spouse do something they don't really want to do?" I trust your answer is no. And meeting in the middle is one solution that can align with who you want to be as individuals and as a couple.

REFLECTIONS

- What comes up for you when you think about making it a goal to meet in the middle? What are some examples of where this really worked well for you? What made them work well? What was good about how you both approached each situation? How can you keep that in mind for other issues where it's harder to meet in the middle?

- Can you think of a time when it wasn't a good idea to meet in the middle? What happened? What made it hard? What adjustments would you make if you were doing it again? Was the disappointment really about the idea of compromising, or was it more about the actual compromise you reached? Why?

WORKING TOGETHER THIS WEEK

☐ Who in this marriage is more likely to be willing to compromise? How do you know? How does it feel if you're making the most compromises? What do you want your spouse to know and understand? How does it feel to be with a partner who is quick to meet you in the middle?

☐ This week, give yourself a meet in the middle challenge. Be intentional to find ways to compromise and work well together, even when you initially want to approach things differently. Notice how easy or hard it is for you to keep this in mind and make the necessary adjustment.

☐ Pray this week that God will help you have a "meet in the middle" mindset. Ask Him to show you where you and your spouse are already on the same page about many important things. Invite His wisdom into the places where you are in conflict, and receive His insight as to how you can be at peace with each other while you figure it out.

OWNING YOUR PRIORITIES

For where your treasure is, there your heart
will be also.

LUKE 12:34

When I'm coaching couples, I often notice how one or both of them
will want their partner to prioritize the things that are important to
them. For example, one person may be tidy, and the other person is
less so. Because the tidy person values putting things in their place,
they expect their spouse to value it at the same level. But this is rarely
the case, and instead of just owning their priority and thus taking
responsibility for it, they spend a lot of time trying to get their spouse
to be tidier.

When I teach the concept of owning your priorities, you get the
opportunity to love the things that are important to you. You get
to give a full, hearty yes to them. And when it comes to daily living
tasks, you do not need your partner to also say yes. Many couples
get stuck with the idea of what things "should" be like, but I want to
empower you to create scenarios that can really work for you.

In your marriage, there will be things that you will have to take
care of on your own. Not all tasks will be jointly shared. Decide now
that this is okay, and you will avoid a lot of unnecessary conflict.
This verse reminds us that we cannot always project our standards
onto others. You can feel good about the things that are priorities for
you and accept your spouse wherever they land on the issues. This
perspective will help you avoid so much tension and strife because
of your differences.

REFLECTIONS

- What are your thoughts about owning your priorities? In what instances can this idea really work for you as a couple? Where might it be more difficult? Why? What ways could you make it work? What's gained if you see it this way? What are you afraid will be lost?

- Reflect on a time when you were proud about something you took full responsibility for. What made you feel this way? Did anyone notice or acknowledge your effort? What impact did that have on you? How might you apply what you learned from that to your marriage?

WORKING TOGETHER THIS WEEK

☐ What are two things one of you prioritizes and the other does not as much? How have you navigated these differences? What bumps along the way have you encountered? How can you take more ownership of this area without feeling resentful? What would be the benefit of doing that?

☐ Knowing the differences between you, how can you decide now how you will react and respond when it feels like your priorities are clashing? What do you want to always remember? How can God help you see these situations on a higher level? What if your goal was to make Him proud and not convince your spouse to be different?

☐ Together, identify your top two priorities as individuals and share why they are so important to each of you right now. Also discuss if and when those priorities might shift and what other aspects of your life might become more important. Exchange ideas for how you can support each other, even if your priorities are different at the moment.

SETTING BOUNDARIES

All you need to say is simply "Yes" or "No";
anything beyond this comes from the evil one.

MATTHEW 5:37

How often do you find yourself agreeing to do things that you really don't want to do? I'm not talking about the responsibilities of "adulting" but about things that you agree to because you don't want to upset or disappoint others. Many times, we find ourselves piling things upon our plates to help others, but at the expense of our own well-being.

It may come as a surprise to you, but this happens a lot in marriage as well. Many people decades into a marriage come to realize they have completely lost themselves because much of their time together has been seeking each other's approval without first assessing if they have their own approval. As you start your marriage, it's important that you know what is a hard "yes" and what is a hard "no" for you. Setting boundaries can be an act of love for yourself and an act of honor for your partner.

Some struggle with saying no in a way that they perceive as nice. I personally have struggled with this in my own life. But a mentor once shared that you can be kind and respectful without having to be "nice." This means you can just be clear with yourself about what you will do and what doesn't work for you. The more comfortable you get with this idea in your marriage, the more authentic relationship you'll have together. God made you both unique, and it's not necessary or healthy to become carbon copies of each other.

REFLECTIONS

- Boundaries are different from ultimatums or threats. Boundaries protect you and your interests, whereas ultimatums are attempts to try to control what someone else does. When was a time you set a boundary in your relationship? When was a time you might have given your spouse an ultimatum or made a threat of some sort?

- What are boundaries you feel very clear on? What are boundaries where there might be some gray areas? How can you be clearer with yourself about what is a yes and what is a no for you?

WORKING TOGETHER THIS WEEK

☐ Rate your ability to set boundaries on a scale from 1 to 10 (where 1 is not at all and 10 is very much). What comes up for you when you think about this, and what messages did you receive growing up about saying yes or no to certain things? Does it seem easier or harder to set boundaries in your marriage when compared to other relationships?

☐ What can you do to make it easier to talk about boundaries together as a couple? Share with each other two things you are willing to give so that your communication on these topics can be productive rather than creating conflict. For example, you may offer to listen before reacting or dismissing your partner's needs, or to ask clarifying questions before making assumptions.

☐ How can you support each other in being authentic? How can you and your partner express your desires clearly without fear of judgment? Can you think of any times when you might have subtly pressured the other person to be more like you in one area? How did they respond?

DE-ESCALATING ARGUMENTS

If a ruler's anger rises against you, do not leave
your post; calmness can lay great offenses
to rest.

ECCLESIASTES 10:4

There will be times in your marriage when conversations escalate
to arguments. When you notice this happening, I want you to be
prepared and equipped with tools that will help you create a sense of
calmness and end your discussion in a way that feels productive. It's
important to note that it takes two people to create an argument, two
people who are so committed to their own perspective that they will
avoid listening.

Even if in the moment, one of you is getting angry, the other can
choose to follow the direction of this scripture. Imagine when you
are upset being met with calmness—there's not much to fuel the
fire of your anger. Even the notion of "not leaving your post" is wise
instruction. As I think about your goals for your marriage, it's almost
as if God is saying, "Don't forget what you're here to do. Don't forget
what all this is about in the first place."

I often chuckle when I read the Bible and see just how much God
Himself was a life coach. The Bible is a wonderful manual for how
to navigate every single issue you will face as a human being on this
earth—and as a couple together in Christ. Every type of relationship
is illustrated, and in your marriage, you will have various interactions
that mirror these relationships.

REFLECTIONS

- In this scripture, there is reference made to a ruler—indicating a person in power who is angry. How would you describe the power dynamics in your relationship? How do you feel about it? Which one of you is more likely to be angry, and which one is more likely to remain calm? How are you making your different temperaments work?

- Reflect on a time when you were able to stay focused on the larger goal at hand, even in the midst of a conflict. What helped you do that? How did your choices impact the conversation?

WORKING TOGETHER THIS WEEK

☐ Discuss together two types of situations in your marriage in which you find yourself easily offended. What are you doing to manage your reactions to these situations? Why do you think you get upset about these things? Keeping the goal of your marriage in mind, how can your spouse calmly respond to you?

☐ Thank each other for a time when your anger was met with calmness. What were you so angry about? How did your spouse's calmness impact you? Did it help you calm down, or were you even more upset that they were calm? What would have happened if they had been just as angry as you?

☐ Pray for each other on the topic of calmness. What would you like God to do for you and your spouse in this area? What will be different in your relationship when this prayer is answered? What if God has already answered it? What would you do differently in the coming week?

MANAGING YOUR EMOTIONS

In your anger do not sin: Do not let the sun go
down while you are still angry.

EPHESIANS 4:26

God has given us all a range of emotions. In our society, we are taught that some emotions are good and some are bad. I like to think of emotions as teachers, and in that regard all of them have value. How we feel is an indication of how we think. And if we don't like the way we are feeling, we need only go to how we are thinking to make the change.

In this scripture, we are confronted with the emotion of anger. Notice that the verse does not instruct us not to get angry, only not to sin. What God is telling us is that it's okay to feel angry. We are human. Things will go wrong, and people will let us down. Yet we are still held to a certain standard of behavior and conduct. We are instructed not to sin and to not let our anger turn into resentment.

I think many times people take the recommendation of not letting the sun go down quite literally. In some instances, that may be the wisest choice. In others, it is helpful to take a break and revisit a conversation later. I think the goal here is to make sure you don't get into the habit of sweeping things under the rug and pretending not to be upset even when you are. Notice the things that separate you as a couple. If anger is one of them, commit yourselves to finding productive ways to manage this emotion better.

REFLECTIONS

- Consider some of the emotions that are traditionally considered negative, such as sadness, loneliness, anger, frustration, and disappointment. What if they are there to teach you something about yourself or about what you actually want? What message would they be conveying to you, and how could you use these emotions to guide your marriage in a positive way?

- How often do you feel angry? What are your thoughts about it? How do you typically operate when you are angry—do you hold it in or release it quickly? Would you consider your reactions and behavior as sinful? What would God want you to do in these moments?

WORKING TOGETHER THIS WEEK

☐ Together, come up with an anger-management plan. This is the list of things you will do for yourself or in support of each other so that you do not sin against each other in your anger. If you see yourself as a team working on this and taking care of your marriage baby, how would you do that?

☐ Have there been times when you have given the devil a foothold because you were so angry and thinking negatively about each other? Now that you've had some distance from that experience, what would you say in defense of your spouse and in protection of your marriage?

☐ What are some healthy ways to express your anger? Make a list of three to five things you can do to release any angry feelings without damaging your relationship.

END ON A GOOD NOTE

I have fought the good fight, I have finished the
race, I have kept the faith.

2 TIMOTHY 4:7

How fitting that we come to the end of this part of the book and read a scripture that talks about a "good fight." We don't often see it this way. Most people try to avoid conflict or see it as bad. There are definitely moments when it puts a strain on the connection. But it is not something to be dismissed as unhelpful.

I believe that conflict in marriage can be healthy and in some ways is necessary. When you have conflict, you come to understand yourself better—what matters to you, what position you hold, or how you see the world. And in the conflict you also learn the same about your spouse. In fact, you can consider conflict as you and your spouse coming together to discuss two different perspectives and ideas.

As Believers, you don't ever have to be the referee of who is wrong and who is right. God is the ultimate judge. But you can have productive conflict that brings you closer.

As you reflect on this week's scripture, have you considered what is worth fighting for? What would be your good fight? How could you have a disagreement with your spouse and still be in faith? Marriage conflicts are usually values conflicts. When you keep God in the center and align yourself with His values, coming together in marriage becomes much easier.

REFLECTIONS

- What does it look like for you to finish the race as a couple? What will you have achieved together? What might you have achieved individually? How do you see yourself contributing to your finishing the race together?

- Reflect on a time when conflict was healthy and productive and served your marriage in positive ways. What were the outcomes of that conflict? What did you learn about yourself and your spouse? How have those times influenced how you handle conflict now?

WORKING TOGETHER THIS WEEK

☐ Write down a list of indicators for when you know you are having productive conflict. What is happening in your conversations in these instances? What are the things that are not happening? How can you begin to acknowledge and even celebrate when you have productive, healthy conflict?

☐ In your journey together, what are the things you want to "keep the faith" about? What would potentially test your faith in these areas? How can you be conscious to grow and stretch your faith as a couple? What are two things you could do in the coming months?

☐ How can God best support you in handling conflict with grace? Let Him see your heart on this matter. Pray for yourself and each other that you will be mindful of the things He wants you to know and see. Keep track of the new insights you have after praying.

OUR FAITHFUL JOURNEY

What will be the easiest devotion from this part of the book to apply in your marriage? The hardest? What surprised you the most? Explain why.

EXPRESSING LOVE WITH ABUNDANCE

In part 4, we will explore the abundance of love available to us through our relationship with God. His love flows through us so that we can love each other well. We will find many similarities between how God loves us and how you and your spouse love each other as we consider what you want love to look like in your marriage.

THE ABUNDANCE OF GOD'S LOVE

And so we know and rely on the love God has
for us. God is love. Whoever lives in love lives
in God, and God in them.

1 JOHN 4:16

God is the foundation of love. And it is through Him that you will love each other well in your marriage. Because God is love, connecting to Him is connecting to love. In essence, you live in love. Imagine it being the air around you. You inhale it just by being alive. It's always available to you as a Believer.

Because God so generously pours out His love for and onto you, you can operate in the overflow of His love. This means that you are always loved and have love to give to your spouse and those around you. There is no end to the love available to you through God. Even when you perceive that your spouse may not be loving you the way you would like or to the degree you would like, you always have God's love to fill in the gaps. You don't ever have to go through the experience of being "unloved" because that is an impossible state with God.

You can always rely on God's love. If your love fails, God's love will take over. If you find yourself struggling to love the way God loves, that's okay. You don't have to rely on your own strength. Accessing God's love is as a simple as asking for it. He has promised in His word: "Ask and it will be given to you; seek and you will find; knock and the door will be opened to you" (Matthew 7:7). That's a promise, always kept.

REFLECTIONS

- How often do you find yourself relying on God's love? In what situations is this easy for you to do? When do you find it most difficult? What difference does it make when you are able to rely on God's love? What's the impact in your life?

- Think about a time when you felt like you could not access God's love the way you wanted to. What was happening? What was getting in the way? What were you thinking about yourself? About God? How might some of those same thoughts and experiences come up in your marriage?

WORKING TOGETHER THIS WEEK

- [ ] Read Ephesians 3:17–19 together. What do you understand about the depth of God's love for you as individuals? Now consider that same love for you as a couple and for your marriage. How does knowing how much God loves your union influence the way you think about it?

- [ ] What does it look like for you to be able to operate from the abundance of God's love as a couple? What are things you would be thinking and doing more regularly? What are things you'd be thinking and doing less often?

- [ ] Spend a few moments writing a love letter to God. What do you want Him to know about your love for Him? What does His love mean to you as a couple? How has His love already made a difference in your time as a couple?

PURPOSE OF MARRIAGE

May the Lord direct your hearts into God's love and Christ's perseverance.

2 THESSALONIANS 3:5

Marriage is the playground to practice God's love. What if that were its only purpose?

I believe this perspective will serve you well in your marriage. When we look for love to direct us in marriage, we release many unnecessary expectations of and requirements for each other. The success of your marriage becomes more about loving each other well rather than following a list of social norms and expectations that have never been questioned.

When your heart is directed toward love, you embody all the characteristics of love—you are patient and kind, you are not envious, you do not boast, you honor each other, you are selfless, you are not easily angered, you don't hold things against each other (1 Corinthians 13:4–8). This is the essence of what marriage is all about! When you are tempted to make it about anything else but love—like what you are getting, how your spouse should be meeting your needs, how they should be supporting you more—return to love. Ask God to direct your thinking toward love. Let the idea of loving your spouse more be your guide. This may be counterintuitive when you are frustrated and angry with each other, but it is the answer.

Consciously choosing the goal of love in your marriage will require perseverance. It's something you will need to commit to over and over again, even when you don't feel like it. The discomfort will be normal in some instances. But God is there to give you the strength you need, each and every time.

REFLECTIONS

- What would be different if the only expectation you have of yourself in your marriage was to love your spouse at your highest capacity? What would you stop focusing on or worrying about? What would you pay more attention to? How would you know if you were doing a good job?

- How would you describe your relationship to perseverance? What does it look like to persevere in love? Why might that be a helpful concept to consider in a marriage? What might make persevering hard for you? What would make it worth it?

WORKING TOGETHER THIS WEEK

☐ Come up with a fun challenge this week that requires you to persevere as a couple. For example, you might challenge yourselves to drink eight glasses of water a day, to avoid scrolling on your phone after a certain time, or to pray together. Take note of the mindset you have to adopt in order to persevere. Share your observations and reflections with each other at the end of the week.

☐ Think about your perseverance plan as a couple. If things get really hard in your marriage, what five steps are you committed to taking? Are there any circumstances under which you would not follow through on these steps? What are they, and why? What might you do if you are committed to the steps and your spouse is not for whatever reason?

☐ For God to direct your hearts toward love, you must be willing to allow Him to do so. How hard or easy is it for you to open your heart to God's direction when you are angry or hurt?

☐ What shift would you need to make in those instances? Discuss the reasons why you would want to.

DEFINING YOUR LOVE

My command is this: Love each other as I have
loved you.

JOHN 15:12

God's commandment of us is to love. But when we, in our humanity, define what love means from our own understanding, we often miss the mark. There is no greater love than the love God has for us. He is the originator and the purest definition of love. When it comes to defining what it means to love in your marriage, God's example is the place to start. It's not something you need to search all over the world or internet to understand. And in many ways, it's already in you as a child of God.

This scripture invites us to consider the ways God has loved us. What does that mean to you? What has God's love looked like in your life? We know so much about God's love from the Bible. We know that God's love is sacrificial and that it never ends. Think of the safety and security we have knowing that nothing will ever truly separate us from God's love. This promise from Him enables us to show up as ourselves without shame. Think about this in your own marriage and how much of a difference it would make for you to be loved unconditionally.

As you grow together as a couple, keep yourself anchored in the simplicity represented in this verse. You do not need to overcomplicate love. There is an easy peace that comes with it. Your own personal relationship with God will shape your definition of love in your marriage. When your heart is turned toward God and anchored in His example, there is no wrong way to love.

REFLECTIONS

- In what ways does your spouse love you like God loves you? In what ways do you love them like God loves them? How does this make your marriage different from marriages in which people may not know God? Where is there room for you both to grow in how you love each other?

- God actually commands us to love. As our Father, He knows this is what's best for us even when we don't. Think about moments in your life when the best choice was to love. Did you make that choice? Why or why not? What did you learn?

WORKING TOGETHER THIS WEEK

☐ Find your favorite verse in the Bible on the topic of love. Share that scripture with each other and why it is your favorite. Talk through the ways you strive to love each other the way described. Discuss a time when you feel like you received love as described in that scripture. How did that expression of love impact you?

☐ How has God loved you just this week? Write out a list of seven different ways you have received God's love recently. Notice if this is something you think about often and give God praise for or if your list represents things you sometimes take for granted. How can you become even more present to God's love for you on a daily basis?

☐ Together, come up with a simple sentence that represents your definition of love for your marriage. How close are you already coming to this definition? How can God help you get all the way there? Write down your definition and place it somewhere you can both refer to it often.

EXPANDED LOVE

He answered, "Love the Lord your God with all
your heart and with all your soul and with all
your strength and with all your mind."

LUKE 10:27

Many are familiar with the book *The Five Love Languages* by Gary
Chapman. I love that it offers a framework for understanding the
various ways in which we all naturally give and receive love. I think
this book can do a lot of good in relationships. It helps readers
understand themselves and their partners better. It helps bridge the
gap in those moments when one person may not be feeling loved in
the way they would like.

At the same time, I've seen couples use the five love languages
against each other. It's easy for some people to make their love language the demanded language—meaning their spouse now needs
to follow a rule book for how to love them. I want to recommend
that you and your spouse consider the five love languages as love
expanders. They form a guidebook for all the different ways you can
consciously demonstrate your love. Any given way is not "right" or
"wrong": They are all necessary and have their place. That way, you
get to experience love in an expanded capacity.

This scripture speaks about love in its variety of forms. God
is instructing you to love with heart (your emotions), soul (your
consciousness), strength (your will), and mind (your intellect).
Essentially, everything you have. This perspective is helpful when
you think of loving at your full capacity. It requires you to go deeper
than you might normally think about. It all starts with your ability to
love God the way He is instructing here.

REFLECTIONS

- What is your love language? Describe a time when you really felt loved by your partner in this way. Describe a time when you were conscious of showing your love using their preferred love language. What did it feel like to do this if it was not your natural love language?

- Why do you think God instructs us to love this deeply? What would be your motivation for striving to love God in this way? How might that help you love your spouse more? Would you expect or ask that they love you the same way in return? Why or why not?

WORKING TOGETHER THIS WEEK

☐ Identify one way you will expand the way you show love. Why did you pick it? What are the things that typically get in the way of you demonstrating love in this way? How will you keep it at the top of your mind so you are conscious of doing it?

☐ Looking at the preceding scripture, rank on a scale from 1 to 10 (1 is not much and 10 is a great deal) how well you are doing at loving God with all your heart, soul, strength, and mind. Compare your highest and lowest scores. What do you take away from this assessment? Where do you want to focus on doing better? What's one thing you'll do this week?

☐ One way we love is with our feelings. What does it feel like in your body to love your spouse? When did you first notice this feeling? What thoughts or situations are usually associated with your feeling this way?

SACRIFICIAL LOVE

This is love: not that we loved God, but that he loved us and sent his Son as an atoning sacrifice for our sins. Dear friends, since God so loved us, we also ought to love one another.

1 JOHN 4:10–11

I think we all know intellectually that love is sometimes a sacrifice. We want to genuinely believe we will make those sacrifices when called to do so. But making a sacrifice is hard. That's why it's called sacrifice! We are giving up something we deeply desire or treasure for the sake of someone else. And if we are all honest, our human nature does not want to do that at all.

Sacrifice doesn't come when we have an abundance of love to give—it comes when we don't think we have any at all to give. Sacrifice requires a conscious effort, and often it is uncomfortable. We are wired to avoid discomfort, and so everything within us will resist making the sacrifice. Or if we do, we may be tempted to want our spouse to repay us for that sacrifice in some way.

But how wonderful that God does not operate that way. His sacrifice is genuine. He gave the hardest thing in the world to give. Can you imagine the agony and pain that must have caused? And yet He did it willingly. He doesn't ask us to do the same thing for Him. A love like that is contagious, and out of respect and reverence for His love, we are compelled to love Him and others. We don't have to sacrifice our lives to do that. Often it only requires that we sacrifice our pride and ego. Consider making that sacrifice more often than you might want and more often than is comfortable. The rewards of a sacrificial love are never-ending. God is proof of that for us.

REFLECTIONS

- When you hear the word "sacrifice," what are your immediate reactions? Does it make you cringe, or are you open to it? What's a great sacrifice you've already made in your marriage? Do you think your partner is aware of this sacrifice? How does that impact you?

- When you think about how much God loved you, even before you ever loved Him, what comes up for you? Why do you think He loves you so much? Do you ever struggle to feel worthy of that sacrifice? How can you assure yourself that in God's eyes, you are already worthy?

WORKING TOGETHER THIS WEEK

☐ Notice all the small and big sacrifices you make this week—not only in your marriage but in other areas of life. Do you consider yourself a person who regularly makes sacrifices? Is there one area of life where you find yourself sacrificing more than others? Are there some sacrifices you feel count more than others? Why or why not?

☐ Aside from God, who is someone in your life who has made huge sacrifices for you? Do you think you have appropriately expressed your gratitude for their sacrifices? How could you express even more appreciation this week, even if the sacrifices were made a long time ago?

☐ Sometimes sacrifices go unnoticed because we are just not aware. Many times this is unintentional. How can you be more conscious to notice your spouse's sacrifices? How can you let them know the things that you really want acknowledged?

CAPACITY TO GIVE

And hope does not put us to shame, because
God's love has been poured out into our
hearts through the Holy Spirit, who has been
given to us.

ROMANS 5:5

As children, we first learn about love from our parents or guardians. We come to understand what love looks like and feels like based on how we are loved, treated, and cared for in our homes. Depending on the emotional health of the people raising us, either we form secure, loving attachments and are able to easily express love, or we form insecure, anxious attachments and are shut off to some forms of love.

It's important to truly understand just how much one's upbringing influences the way they are able to love. Many times in a marriage, people can question their own worthiness to receive love. If their partner is not as attentive, doting, and complimentary, they may wonder if they are a lovable person. They may ask, "What's wrong with me that they can't love me more fully?" It may be that their partner is stunted in their ability to *give* love.

When you give love based on how it was given to you, there will always be lack, and your capacity to give it in your marriage is limited. But when you can recognize and receive God's abundant love, which is literally "poured out into our hearts," you see just how your ability to give love is never-ending. No matter how much love you did or did not receive as a child, you can, through the Holy Spirit, also pour out your love onto your spouse. It may feel unfamiliar and uncomfortable at times, but God wants your heart to be filled with love so you can give it freely, knowing there is always more.

REFLECTIONS

- Think back to how love was expressed to you as a child. Did it feel abundant or scarce? How do you think your upbringing has impacted the way you are able to give love as an adult? Do you ever find yourself not sure of how to give love, or is it something you feel is natural and easy for you to do?

- What is it like for you to give love to your spouse? Is it something you are intentional about, or does it feel natural? If it's natural, what contributes to that? Can you imagine a time when it might not feel natural and you might have to be more intentional? What are your thoughts about those potential instances?

WORKING TOGETHER THIS WEEK

☐ If you were to write a love letter to your childhood self, what would you say? What would you want your younger self to know about genuine love? Whom would you want that child to model their love on? How would life be different for you if you were able to apply what you know now to yourself back then?

☐ How would you rate your capacity to give love on a scale from 1 to 10 (where 1 is very low and 10 is extremely high)? Why did you give it that rating? What would it look like if you were a 10? What are the things that get in the way of you being a 10? What is one action step you could take this week to move you higher on the scale?

☐ Who is someone you know who is able to give love freely? What is it like to be around this person? How do you feel? What do you think about their generosity of love? Why do you think they are like that? What benefits do you think they get from loving so abundantly? This week, be sure to let them know how much you appreciate their love.

CAPACITY TO RECEIVE

But because of his great love for us, God, who
is rich in mercy, made us alive with Christ even
when we were dead in transgressions—it is by
grace you have been saved.

EPHESIANS 2:4–5

Are you good at receiving gifts? Do you welcome and appreciate
people's generosity, or is doing so uncomfortable for you? In a healthy
marriage, there is a balance between giving and receiving love. When
your marriage feels one-sided, there is fertile ground for resentment
to grow—both for the person who is giving and feels unappreciated
because their partner is not a good receiver and for the person who is
receiving but feels smothered and overwhelmed by their partner's love.

You will know if you are good at receiving when you look at your
willingness to ask for help. If you are used to doing things on your
own or if you are the person other people turn to for help, asking for
someone else's assistance may feel very foreign to you. When I'm
coaching my clients, especially the ones with small children, this is
a topic we dive into regularly. One partner is overwhelmed trying to
take care of everything but does not ask for the help they need for
fear of feeling guilty and too demanding.

God wants you to be helped. It is not a sign of weakness. In your
marriage, He created you to be interdependent. You are designed
to support and help each other in specific ways. Help can be a
demonstration of love, even when you feel you don't deserve it. This
scripture is a reminder of just how much God extends grace to us
and we receive things not because of our own doing but because
He loves us that much. The generous outpouring of love and help
offered to you by your spouse is their gift to you. Take it as such.

REFLECTIONS

- What is it like to sit with the reality of "God's great love" for you? Is that something you believe you have fully received? Why or why not? If you have not yet fully received it, what else needs to happen inside you in order to be able to do so?

- How do you respond to your spouse's generosity toward you? Is it something you expect, or would you rather they didn't overextend themselves? Notice the connection between your ability to give and your ability to receive love in your marriage. What themes do you see?

WORKING TOGETHER THIS WEEK

☐ This week, practice receiving love and help from your partner. Think of three things you'd like them to consider. Make the request, and if they say yes, be a gracious receiver. Do you think this will be easy or hard for you? Why? What does it bring up for you?

☐ Stretch yourself to also receive from other people in your life. This may be simple things like graciously receiving a compliment, a smile, or even a hello. Pay attention to how you feel receiving things from your spouse versus people you know less well.

☐ Lastly, notice all the ways God is giving His love to you as a couple this week. Write down all the "gifts" and blessings you receive from Him. What is it like for you to jointly receive from Him? How does your spouse's ability to receive affect your ability and comfort in receiving?

COST OF WITHHOLDING

There is no fear in love. But perfect love drives
out fear, because fear has to do with punish-
ment. The one who fears is not made perfect
in love.

1 JOHN 4:18

Tell me if this sounds familiar: "If you don't ... then I won't ..." It's
human nature to make decisions around what we do based on what
someone else does. It feels risky to give of ourselves when we don't
feel that someone else is giving equally. There may be times in your
marriage when you are angry, hurt, sad, or frustrated, and in an
effort to protect yourself, you will want to build up a wall around
your heart and withhold love and kindness from your spouse. Your
brain will tell you all the reasons why to hold back, keep to yourself,
and stop making the effort. It's a lie from the enemy to keep you
stuck and feeling bad toward each other.

When you notice yourself wanting to withhold love from your
spouse, question it. Ask yourself, why am I doing this? What benefit
do I get from not loving in this moment? What am I sacrificing when
I think I am protecting myself? Withholding your love always comes
at a cost. And when you realize just how costly it is to your own
well-being and fulfillment, you will think twice about it.

As this scripture tells us, any withholding of love comes from
fear. We are afraid of being hurt more or afraid of investing in
something that doesn't give us the return we expect. But love is an
abundant asset, and there is never a time when we give love that it
doesn't come back to us. It may take longer than we expect, but it
always magnifies itself.

REFLECTIONS

- Reflect on a time when you withheld your love from your spouse or someone else. What was going on with you in that situation? What did you want from the other person that you felt like you were not getting? What was the cost to you for withholding love and kindness? How did they respond to you?

- Given what you know about love and God's love, why do you think there is no fear in love? What does fear represent? What does love represent? Why might it be possible for love to cast out fear?

WORKING TOGETHER THIS WEEK

☐ Share with your spouse two things you are afraid of that cause you to withhold your love. What would you need to think in order for this to no longer be a fear or concern for you? How could your spouse support you more in this?

☐ Take your fears to God in prayer. Ask Him to help you understand where they come from and to give you the insight that you have nothing to fear. Invite Him to open your eyes to the safety and security you can always find in Him.

☐ Discuss together what it means to be made perfect in love. What would it feel like? What things would you be thinking more often? What are things you would do for yourself and each other? Decide one thing you will think or do this week in an effort to operate at a higher level of love.

DECIDING TO LOVE

As the Father has loved me, so have I loved you. Now remain in my love.

JOHN 15:9

This verse represents such a simple equation. Father has loved the Son. The Son has loved you. Remain in that love. Seems easy enough, right? But how many times have we felt disconnected from God's love, either from Him directly or from His love that flows through others? How many times have we felt like we don't have access to that love in order to give it to others? I want to offer that it's not that the love is absent, it's that you have consciously or unconsciously decided *not* to choose it.

Deciding to love is a conscious decision to override programming, conditioning, and limiting beliefs that would have you believe you can't love, shouldn't love, or don't have love to give. Deciding to love can be a nonnegotiable in your life. It can be something you commit to doing ahead of time. In fact, when you said your wedding vows, that's essentially what you were doing. Deciding to love. No matter what.

The way we do that is by remaining in the flow of God's love. Imagine it is a current always there. We step into and out of it. But when you decide to love, you keep stepping into it, even when other situations or negative thinking will try to lure you away. There will be times in your marriage when loving is an act of your will. But God has already given you the power to overcome and "take captive" any thought that would take you out of love (2 Corinthians 10:5).

REFLECTIONS

- Whether we are aware of it or not, we choose our emotions all the time. Our emotions are driven by the thoughts we tell ourselves. When you are not choosing and deciding to love, what are you choosing instead?

- This verse, "Now remain in my love," in some ways sounds like a loving directive. As a parent might admonish a child to "stay over there," it's a direction of protection. How is God trying to protect you by instructing you to remain in His love?

WORKING TOGETHER THIS WEEK

☐ What does it mean for you to remain in God's love as a couple? How would you complete this sentence? "Remaining in God's love is when . . ." What are two things that can throw you off sometimes? How do you want to navigate those moments together as a couple?

☐ Be intentional about deciding to love your spouse this week. What is one thing you can be more conscious about? Think of two reasons you would want to decide to demonstrate your love in this way. How will it feel to make a powerful decision from a place of love?

☐ Remaining in God's love requires commitment. What things do you find yourself easily able to commit to no matter what? Identify two common themes and then apply them to your commitment to remain in God's love.

GOD'S LOVE CONQUERS ALL

Above all, love each other deeply, because love
covers over a multitude of sins.

1 PETER 4:8

It is God's love that has covered our sins and shortcomings. It is His love that is able to help us in times of weakness. It is His love that finds no fault in us. And this same love can operate in your marriage. It may be a cliché that love conquers all, but that's only when you have a limited view of love. When we take the perspective of God's love, we have an entirely new perspective.

Human love is fallible and fails. God love is infallible and never fails. Human love is conditional and inconsistent. God's love is unconditional and always consistent. Human love is often dependent on our own strength. God's love knows no bounds. So, yes, God's love does in fact conquer all—you just have to access it.

It's important to note that although God's love covers all, we are still allowed to have standards and boundaries. We can love someone and also do things to protect ourselves if their actions are not loving toward us. Love is a conscious decision to accept where someone is and to have compassion. It means you can forgive and not hold things against each other. It means you can be healed from your own hurt caused by the actions of someone else. But it does not mean you continue to allow yourself to be victimized or mistreated in any way. God's love can shepherd you toward any help you may need, whether that is from a trusted friend, a pastor, or professional support. By honoring your values and protecting your boundaries, you are manifesting the highest vision of His love for you.

REFLECTIONS

- Do you personally believe that God's love conquers all? Why or why not? How does your belief shape the way you experience certain situations? How does it impact the way you experience God?

- Reflect on a time when someone's love covered your sin. Perhaps you made a mistake or a bad choice. How did the love and understanding you received impact you? What were you feeling inside after you realized the mistake? What did you think of yourself? In what ways did the love you receive help you feel better?

WORKING TOGETHER THIS WEEK

☐ This week, pray that God's love would help you let go of something you've held on to. Perhaps it's something your spouse did or said that impacted you negatively. Invite God in to heal that hurt, and let His love make up for their actions. Spend time thinking about what it will be like to let love cover it all. What will now be available to you when you let this go?

☐ Thank your spouse for the way they love you despite your mistakes and shortcomings. Let them know how much you appreciate their patience, understanding, and compassion for you in challenging moments.

☐ Write a note of forgiveness to yourself. Let God's love flow through you so that you can no longer harbor any guilt or shame for anything you've done wrong. Practice self-compassion by saying three kind things to yourself when you are reminded of your mistakes.

PROTECTING
YOUR UNION

"Though the mountains be shaken and the hills be removed, yet my unfailing love for you will not be shaken nor my covenant of peace be removed," says the Lord, who has compassion on you.

ISAIAH 54:10

The union of a marriage is made stronger when it is rooted in the strength of the Lord. Situations and circumstances will come to rock the foundation you have established together. Your love and commitment to each other are to be protected.

This week's verse is a wonderful example of what that looks like. Imagine chaos and challenges you may be confronted with. Loss, transitions, failed plans, desires delayed. These things will bring emotional challenges and heartache. But when you encounter these trials with an eye toward protecting your love as a sacred, precious gift, you approach them differently. You don't blame each other; you support each other. You don't judge each other; you understand each other. You don't withdraw from each other; you lean into each other.

Protecting your love means that anything can be happening in the outside world but you, your spouse, and God live in your own bubble. You can look at certain situations and speak faith, hope, and love into them. You don't doubt your stability as a couple—you get more certain about it. Just as nothing can separate you from the love of God, you decide that nothing will separate you as a couple. This is a powerful decision to make and will dramatically change the way you navigate life's inevitable ups and downs.

REFLECTIONS

- In what ways have you already had to protect your love as a couple? What things have you encountered together that might have thrown you off? What role did each of you play in protecting the love you have established together?

- Reflect on the promise God makes in this verse. What is the emotion you sense behind it? How do these words impact you? When you believe God in this way, how do you respond to challenges that come about to dismantle your peace?

WORKING TOGETHER THIS WEEK

☐ Create your own love protection plan. Just like if you have an alarm in your home, what signals will you send out to alert each other when things are feeling off? What support will you access? What will be some of your immediate steps? And then what will you do to maintain that bubble of protection should things get challenging again?

☐ God has promised you a covenant of peace. What are some concerns and worries you can decide now to place under that covenant? What will need to happen in order for you to continually leave them there under God's protection? It may be helpful to write them down and then symbolically place them in God's hands.

☐ Spend some time thanking God for His unfailing love. Imagine it is an umbrella that is constantly shielding you from the rain and storms of life. You are walking through them, but they are not getting to you. If you find yourself getting wet and too consumed with them, ask God to help you get back under His umbrella.

KEEPING HIS COVENANT

Know therefore that the Lord your God is God;
he is the faithful God, keeping his covenant of
love to a thousand generations of those who
love him and keep his commandments.

DEUTERONOMY 7:9

One thousand generations. Can you even imagine? God is so faithful to His word. Is there anything in the world you could imagine being committed to for one thousand generations? I'm not sure we can genuinely comprehend it. Yet God can say that with boldness and certainty. He knows that He cannot lie. He says what he means and means what He says. What assurance we have in that.

In marriage, if we operate with even a fraction of that level of commitment, things will be absolutely incredible. You don't have to doubt if your spouse will love you forever or if they will always be there for you. It's already established that they will. You could both operate with great freedom when you know that you both are fully committed to love. This verse provides the perfect perspective for you to create that.

God is able to do these things because He decides that He will. His word establishes it as *truth*. There is no option for Him to question it. This certainty is also available to you when you open yourself up to it. Even though all couples make promises and vows to each other, we are human, and there will be times when a thought of "I'm not so sure ..." or "I don't know ..." will surface. Expect these moments to come. And then also know that you can still remain committed just by making the decision to do so.

REFLECTIONS

- God will supersede any commitment you have to Him. In this verse, we see that His promise stands for those who love Him and keep His commandments. Why do you think that is the case? How well do you think you are doing in these areas?

- What's the longest time you've been committed to something? Now imagine being committed a thousand times longer. What would you need to think about? How would you operate knowing you needed to maintain this level of commitment? How can that mindset apply to your marriage?

WORKING TOGETHER THIS WEEK

☐ Think about the impact on your family if the love you establish now will stand for one thousand generations. How does that change things for you? What legacy of love do you want to make sure is passed down the line? What do you want them to know about you and the ways you chose to love?

☐ Write a brief love note to members of future generations who will be looking at your love as a model. What do you want them to always keep in mind? How do you want them to define commitment? What do they need to remember when they face challenges?

☐ Pray that God continues to strengthen your commitment to each other. Imagine that each day you get a new supply of commitment. It never runs out. It's always available to you. How does this realization influence the way you show up and love each other?

FOREVER LOVE

Give thanks to the God of heaven. His love
endures forever.

PSALM 136:26

Forever. What things in life can you truly say last forever? All throughout this part of the devotional, we have been looking at God's love from many different angles. It's through His love that you are able to give, receive, decide, and commit to loving each other well. And as this scripture reminds us, that kind of love can endure forever.

When you think about forever, it has a way of making everything else insignificant. This includes the day-to-day challenges of a marriage. If your spouse unthinkingly says something insensitive, forgets to follow through on something important, or isn't showing up exactly the way you think they should, you can still choose to see your spouse in the light of God's enduring love.

When it comes to trying to conceptualize forever, my mind immediate goes to the end of time here on this earth. I think of what I will value and care about. I think about what will matter the most. The answer for me is simple: love. Have I loved as deep, as long, and as hard as I could have? Did I choose love as often as it was available to me? Did I lean into it when I was hurting, angry, and uncomfortable? Did those I loved the most actually feel love from me? Did I live a life of love? Did I exist in the energy of love? I can't say that I have done these things perfectly. None of us has. But God's love enables us to love forever. I'll take it. I'll work with that. And you can, too.

REFLECTIONS

- What comes up for you when you think about the concept of forever? Does it feel vast and expansive or pressured and overwhelming? Whatever comes up for you, why do you think that is? Is there anyone in your life you truly believe will love you forever?

- Why do you think God wants us to know this? What purpose does knowing He will love you forever have in your life? How does it make your life better? What does it offer you as you go about your day or your year?

- There are many movie titles and songs with "forever" in the title. If you were to create a title for your marriage that incorporated the word "forever," what would it be? Be creative and have fun as you brainstorm ideas.

WORKING TOGETHER THIS WEEK

- ☐ How can you show up more with an attitude of a "forever love"? What things would you be more able to let go of? Where would you start focusing more of your attention?

- ☐ Imagine you are 99 years old. What are the things that would matter to you personally as you consider the concept of love? How can you live more of your life now in accordance with those ideas and values? How can your spouse be helpful? In what ways can you rely on God to help you?

OUR FAITHFUL JOURNEY

Taking into consideration everything you have read in this part
of the book, what is love in abundance? What three things are
essential ingredients for you?

_____

_____

_____

_____

_____

_____

_____

_____

_____

_____

_____

_____

_____

_____

_____

_____

_____

_____

LIFTING YOUR LOVE TO NEW HEIGHTS

Congratulations on completing this devotional! Your investment of time and energy will create amazing experiences over the life of your marriage. The new perspectives and ideas you generated will be with you for life. As you continue to live in the fullness of love that God has for you, remember this devotional is a forever resource. Keep it close and revisit devotions as your marriage grows and transitions.

God has already blessed you in the reading and applying of this book. May you rest assured that your marriage is protected and that He is continuing to do a good work in both of you. He will perfect all things concerning you, and your marriage will thrive not only for years but also in the generations to come after you. Be blessed in your forever journey together.

INDEX

ACKNOWLEDGMENTS

I am grateful to God for the opportunity to be used to deliver this message. I want to acknowledge the countless couples I have worked with and the authentic ways they show up to our work together. It is through their honesty and transparency that I gather the wisdom and insight to share this information and perspective with you.

I am eternally grateful for my family members, who continue to support me in serving you. I am also appreciative of my friends, who encourage me and remind me of the value of this work.

ABOUT THE AUTHOR

Dr. Chavonne Perotte is a life and marriage coach who helps couples love each other well and create healthy, happy marriages. She provides virtual coaching to couples all over the world seeking a combination of Christian-faith guidance and transformational coaching tools.

She received her doctorate from the Johns Hopkins Bloomberg School of Public Health and focused her research on communication and intimate partnerships. She is the author of two books, *Voices in Your Ear: New Conversations to Transform Your Mind and Renew Your Marriage* and *Premarital Workbook for Christians*, in addition to this one. To learn more, to access free resources, and to work with Dr. Chavonne directly, visit her website at DrChavonne.com. You can also follow her on Instagram at @chavonneperotte.